THE
DUNLOP
P.E. HANDBOOK

(An A-Z of Physical Education)

PUBLISHED 1971 BY:
EDUCATION SECTION
DUNLOP LIMITED
25 ST. JAMES'S STREET
LONDON
SW1

D0230140

CONTENTS

Cover illustration, 'Children's Games' by Peter Bruegel (the elder), is reproduced by kind permission of the Kunsthistoriches Museum in Vienna.

FOREWORD

BY THE RT. HON. PHILIP NOEL-BAKER
PRESIDENT, INTERNATIONAL COUNCIL ON
SPORT AND PHYSICAL EDUCATION (UNESCO)

This book has been written for teachers of Physical Education, by teachers of Physical Education, under the editorial direction of Mr. Don Anthony and Mr. Derek Green. (I put their names in alphabetical order, because neither is primus inter pares; together they have done a splendid bit of work.)

All the way from A to Z they have given hints and information which are based on personal experience, and which teachers of P.E. will not find elsewhere.

A for Ageing : wise words which will make young teachers, to their great benefit, think ten or twenty years ahead. The authors might have added that regular exercise, keeping the muscular system in good order, very notably retards the process of age-ing ; holds off for decades the deterioration which diminishes vigour and the pleasure of being alive. ICSPE research at the highest level has proved that that is true.

L for Lesson Notes and Liveners : some young teachers may think that these, though necessary in other kinds of education, are not needed on the playing field or in the gym. Let them listen to the authors before harsh experience brings conviction that these men are right.

Z for zest : Obvious ? I wonder. I believe many teachers never learn that *every* lesson should be fun, both for the instructor and his class. If this Z paragraph brings that some to every reader, the book, for that alone, will be worthwhile.

One word more. From A to Z teachers will find reflections on the great new theme of "Sport for All". This is the wave of the future. ICSPE has done much to convince the leaders of world sport that in this they have a great responsibility to fulfill. Teachers of P.E. can help; they can make their Members of Parliament and the Government understand that facilities must be provided, and leaders trained, so that people of both sexes and all ages can have their proper share in active sport. In the age of motor transport and automated work, this is vital, if we want to keep our nation great.

Philip Noel-Baker

EDITORIAL

The original idea for this book arose out of a conversation between us (the two editors) concerning the problems a Physical Education teacher has to face. One particular lack, where we felt we might be able to help, was the absence of a specialist handbook. To have such an idea is one thing, deciding how and what is a very different matter, particularly when starting from scratch.

The major problem was who could write it?—In the end a small group of people, all teachers or lecturers in Physical Education, engaged on the Academic Diploma in Education (Theory or Practice—Physical Education option) course at London University (1969-70), decided to accept the challenge. For practical reasons it was decided to produce an A to Z with extensive reference appendices. As tutor to the group one editor (Don Anthony) assumed editorial direction while the other editor (Derek Green) undertook the overall editorial rewrite, which is necessary to provide an even style, and the production into book form. Dunlop Limited undertook the sponsorship of the project and made available staff who were conversant with the techniques of book production.

This then is the first edition of The Dunlop Physical Education Handbook (an A-Z for Physical Education teachers). It does not represent the 'opinion' of any officially structured group or organisation, nor does it speak for the University of London. The aim has been, quite simply, to present useful ideas and information in a simple form, to teachers of Physical Education. It is possible that we have omitted, forgotten, erred or offended—if so we would ask you to bear with us. We hope that we have been informative and stimulating.

We would like to thank the many teachers who made suggestions regarding the contents of the book and all those people within and outside, the teaching profession who were kind enough to read draft texts and proofs.

In an exercise such as this, particularly where a second edition may have to be produced in two or three years' time, it is very necessary for the editors to have a firm idea of the usefulness, weaknesses and strengths of the book. We would, therefore, be grateful to receive any letters commenting on the handbook which should be addressed to:— Physical Education Handbook Editors, c/o Education Section, Dunlop Limited, 25 St. James's Street, London S.W.1.

THE EDITORS

THE DUNLOP P.E. HANDBOOK

EDITORS

DEREK GREEN
Education Officer
Dunlop Limited

DON ANTHONY
Principal Lecturer in P.E.
Avery Hill College of Education

MEMBERS OF THE EDITORIAL GROUP

Monica Evans	Battersea College, London.
Ann Pattison	St. Mary's College, Twickenham, Middx.
Edward Buswell	Whitelands College of Education, London.
Lewis Dawkin-Jones	Kingston College of Further Education, Surrey.
Victor Luscombe	Our Lady's R.C. High School, Lancaster.
James Rand	France Hill School, Camberley, Surrey.
Walter Robinson	Torells C. Secondary School for Boys, Grays, Essex.
Peter Williams	Stockwell College of Education, Bromley, Kent.

ABILITY

If you have ability, use it to show how activities should be performed, remembering that it is the pupils, not yourself, who should be tired at the end of the lesson. In activities where your own performance is not of sufficient demonstration standard, use someone in the class as a demonstrative model. To improve your own performance attend the relevant courses organised by your own authority, by various sports bodies or by the C.C.P.R. at numerous holiday courses.

DEMONSTRATION

ACCIDENTS

Accidents can happen to pupils working even under experienced teachers using the most stringent safety precautions. You can only ensure that you do your best by taking fully adequate safety measures. Most local authorities issue their own safety precautions and it is a *must* to possess a copy, as well as the D.E.S. Booklet "Safety Precautions in Schools". You should have an adequate knowledge of First Aid, and know if anyone else in the school is qualified in First Aid. Always keep a well stocked First Aid kit in a place accessible to others when you have to remain with the accident.

When an accident happens. Clear all people away from the injured person and ascertain immediately the extent of the injuries. Call for advice from anyone better qualified than yourself who is available. Shock should be dealt with initially by words of encouragement and, if the injured pupil can move on his own, get him or her to a place of warmth. If the injury looks serious and the person cannot be moved, keep him or her warm until assistance arrives. If in any doubt, or in case of serious injuries (broken bones etc.), arrange for speedy transfer to hospital by ambulance. Contact the parents to ensure they know first what has happened and record the remedial action that has been taken. Arrange for return transport from the hospital, if applicable. If a pupil is sent to Hospital someone must accompany him or her. Do not attempt to interfere with broken bones or dislocations—you may do more harm than good. With head and eye injuries leave alone until *expert* medical advice arrives.

School Organisation. As soon after the accident as possible fill in an Accident Form, with witnesses' statements attached, for the School Office to forward to the appropriate authority. For your interest, and possible later reference, keep an Accident

Book in which to enter the details of all accidents however minor. In the likelihood of your being involved regarding liability get in touch with your professional association (N.U.T., N.A.S., P.E.A., A.T.C.D.E., B.A.O.L.P.E., etc.)

SAFETY, FIRST AID, LEGALITY, INSURANCE

ACCOMPANISTS

Where movement, dance, dance drama etc. involves the necessity for musical accompaniment, the provision of an accompanist can be a problem which may be dealt with in the following ways :—
1) By integrating the Music and P.E. Depts. for specific sessions, so that the best facilities and personnel of both departments may co-operate to produce the best results.
2) In the event of the above not being possible, utilise the appropriate audio-visual aids to produce the required accompaniments. This may be achieved by :—
   a) use of existing records
   b) pre-recording on tape by an accompanist (within or outside the school).
   c) pre-recording on tape of specific parts of existing records to make a continuous performance (as in an ice-skating programme).

ADMINISTRATION

One of the most important tasks of the Physical Education teacher, particularly if in charge of a large department, is the administration necessary to ensure smooth running and efficiency in regard to :—
1) the composition of the P.E. programme,
2) the co-operation of all members of staff involved
3) the use and maintenance of equipment

The P.E. PROGRAMME
1) Decide on activities to be included in
   a) The School lesson programme
   b) Extra-curricular activities (having first ascertained what help can be obtained from outside the P.E. staff).
2) Draw up a syllabus, having regard to the above, containing :
   a) Aims and objectives of the P.E. programme
   b) Overall content of each activity, general areas to be covered in each year, and basic methods to be adopted where applicable.

3) Draw up a timetable, taking into account number of periods per class and teachers available. Try to show visually what pupils will be doing in each lesson so that they can bring appropriate kit—they will not remember from the beginning to end of term without a reminder on the board.

4) Extra-curricular activities, in the form of school teams, etc., will create a large amount of administrative work regarding the arrangement of matches, transport to away fixtures, possible ways of raising money to pay for transport, refreshments, training etc. A first consideration will be to determine availability of staff to take charge of teams and whether this will be done by:
   a) one member of P.E. staff
   b) each master in charge of team
   c) senior boys assuming responsibilities

5) Competitions within the school are important for the pupils who are not good enough for school teams and adequate provision should be made. These provisions may take the form of inter-house, inter-form or inter-group activities carried out over a specified period or at a particular time such as:—
   a) school games periods
   b) sports or athletics days
   c) swimming galas
   d) potted sports or minor games competitions

CO-OPERATION OF ALL TYPES OF STAFF INVOLVED.

It can be generally assumed that co-operation will be forthcoming from 'specialist' P.E. staff, but, in the case of extra-curricular activities, it is essential that other members of staff should be involved. Otherwise the number of activities will be greatly curtailed and in the extreme, will be limited to those which can be dealt with by the P.E. staff.

It is also important to obtain co-operation from the ground staff, the caretaker and the canteen staff with regard to correct pitches etc., being available at the correct times; changing accommodation available; school being opened outside normal hours (Saturday mornings); playing fields being kept in good condition and put out of action when necessary due to inclement weather; refreshments being made available after matches.

It is, of course, of prime importance to achieve good co-operation with the Headteacher in the allocation of periods, and allowances for equipment.

THE STOCK OF EQUIPMENT AND ITS ADEQUATE MAINTENANCE

A point of overall importance to an efficient P.E. programme. Good stocks must be built up to enable as many pupils as possible to practise an activity at the same time and to cut down the waste of time in "waiting to have a go". The difficulty may be obviated to a certain extent by group work, but an adequate supply of apparatus is very important.

In large schools the question of maintenance is very difficult and to be undertaken properly requires a storeman. This situation is a hope for the future, particularly in a campus situation involving two or three schools. Under the present circumstances, in order to maintain equipment, it is important to take a piece of apparatus out of service as soon as a fault develops (if this is possible) so that it may be sent away for repair before becoming completely useless and irretrievably damaged.

COMMITTEES

ADOLESCENCE

Adolescence is usually defined as the period of transition, from childhood to adult status, which occurs during the later "teenage" years (from 13+ onwards). During this period some pupils become difficult in their approach to life at school due to the physiological changes taking place, and in some cases also due to the problems brought about by a change of status in relationship to parents. Physical education provides an avenue through which pupils can relieve themselves of much of the tension which builds up at this time. It is, therefore, important to involve the pupil as much as possible.

An interesting, enjoyable, physically extending P.E. programme can make all the difference to a pupil's attitude to school life and indirectly affect the attitude and enthusiasm for schooling as a whole. Towards the upper part of the school, many headmasters tend to reduce lesson time for P.E. in favour of examination subjects, a principle that should be resisted as strongly as possible.

Older boys must not be given the impression that they are on their own and 'not to be bothered with'. If possible, more varied and interest arousing activities should be introduced so that pupils may find an energetic, enjoyable *"relaxation"* to help relieve tensions created by examination pressures on top of already existing adolescent problems. At this stage an exercise consciousness should be cultivated so young people come to understand that physical activity should not cease at the end of their academic careers.

GROWTH AND DEVELOPMENT

9

AESTHETIC

An aesthetic appreciation, that is an emotional or mental response to beauty or to something which is pleasing or artistic, is a fundamental qualification of the physical education teacher. Much of his life is involved in a study of movement of all kinds, whether it be in the field of gymnastics, dance, or dance drama. Here an aesthetic appreciation adds to the technical ability to "feel" the faults of a performance. Most important of all, by introducing the aesthetic sense in discussion and demonstration, pupils may be led to realise totally the pleasure of doing something well, e.g. throwing the javelin.

It must be accepted, of course, that to be effective or successful, a performance involving movement does not necessarily have to be aesthetic to the performer. . . .but, it may add appreciably to the result !

AGEING AND ADVANCEMENT

Ageing is of immeasurable importance to all human beings, firstly in the effect it may have on their ability to enact adequately in their situation in life, and secondly, particularly where physical performance is vitally involved, in the effect it may have, to a great degree, on their advancement in their work. A teacher of physical education is a member of this latter group and from the beginning of his career must take this factor into consideration.

Not all teachers carry on teaching P.E. until they retire. One of the main reasons being the deterioration in physical perform- ance through ageing, and a consequent decrease in enthusiasm for teaching the subject. There is, of course, also the lack of opportunity to reach the upper levels of the salary scales in the teaching of P.E. in schools.

A Physical Education teacher must consider and accept the fact that around the age of 40, or even earlier, he or she might lose the desire to carry on teaching the subject alone and in such circumstances an alternative career situation will be needed. This will probably mean :—
   a) teaching a different subject
   b) promotion into the administration area of schools, e.g. Deputy Head or Head, with the necessity for a higher qualification than a Diploma in P.E.
   c) Promotion into the administration of P.E. e.g. County P.E. Adviser, C.C.P.R. etc.

d) transfer into the Teaching Training Area of Higher Education e.g. University P.E. Dept. or College of Education.

As far as c) and d) are concerned, the number of openings represent a very small percentage of those teaching P.E. particularly on the male side, and with the advent of the B.Ed. an added qualification in Education is nearly always required.

Dependent on your aspirations as a Physical Educationist, it is *most important* to ensure that your qualifications will be adequate for your purpose. If they are not, you should make the necessary effort to improve them.

All this is not to say that P.E. Teachers cannot continue with their work until retirement. They can! And when they do, they give great inspiration to others.

QUALIFICATIONS

AIMS

Every Physical Education teacher must have clearly formulated aims and objectives.

BIOLOGICAL — helping every child to reach optimum development, encouraging 'exercise consciousness', and enabling people to experience the total pleasure of 'fitness'.

EDUCATIONAL — so organizing physical education that it contributes to the complete education of the individual, the group and society.

SOCIAL — giving people the opportunity to share the values of sports and games, both as players and spectators; enabling people of both sexes, all ages, all races, and different occupations, the chance to meet each other in a 'play' situation; stimulating creative leisure-time hobbies.

EMOTIONAL — providing 'challenge' and adventure in life; helping people to experience communion with nature and an appreciation of 'conservation', through the media of such activities as water sports, mountain sports, and other outdoor activities.

AESTHETIC — introducing an appreciation of movement, form and balance.

11

ALL PEOPLE

With the general decrease in the number of hours spent at work and the corresponding increase in the time available for leisure activities, it is vitally important that, if a society is not to become a nation of "watchers" or passive spectators with a consequent degeneration in physical health, as many people as possible should be persuaded, or led, to indulge in some form of participation in an enjoyable physical activity. In the U.S.S.R. a programme with this problem in view, is called "Sport for Everybody", in West Germany a similar movement is called "The Second Way" and in the U.S.A. there is "Lifetime Sports", where the whole emphasis is on getting more people to take an active part in sport, not in achieving high standards of performance.

Undoubtedly the primary factor must be "education", followed by the provision of adequate facilities and leadership. It is particularly important to take into account the activities in which all members of a family may be involved.

In our P.E. programme in school we must do our best to interest everyone in one or more activities to such an extent that they want to carry the participation on into adult life. In order to achieve such an end we must:— first, include a sufficient variety of activities, increasing towards the upper end of the school, so that as many individual interests can be catered for as possible; and second, implant a background knowledge and zest for enough activities to cater for changes in interest during adult life brought about by changing social maturity and, in due course, ageing.

Sport For All programmes are in the course of development by UNESCO and the Council For Europe.

JOGGING

AMATEUR STATUS

In the sporting world, amateur status means taking part in an activity for the pleasure of doing so, and not for reward by the payment of *money* for services given, or performances recorded. The definition applies only to the services and performances themselves as money may be accepted by performers for personal expenses involved in actually taking part. Travelling expenses to and from the venue, meals, and accommodation during the period of the activity are allowable. Other expenses may be specially allowed, such as compensation for time lost for absence from work, but rules vary according to the particular sporting association involved and all exigencies regarding expenses are dealt with in the rules and regulations of each sporting body. These rules are under almost constant attack and subsequent review.

It is generally possible for an amateur to compete for prizes in the form of goods without the loss of his or her status. The important qualification is that an individual shall not have taken part as a performer for financial gain. In some sports it is possible to revert from professional to amateur status under special circumstances.

Do not advise, or independently rule, on matters of status without full knowledge of current regulations.

ART OF MOVEMENT

A type of Movement study based on the principles laid down by Rudolph Laban with a specific, annotated, movement terminology. Courses in Movement and Educational Dance are arranged at the Art of Movement Studio, Woburn Hill, Addlestone, Surrey, for one and three years. The Studio is recognised by the Department of Science and Education and students are eligible for grant-aid and secondment.

ASSESSMENT

Perhaps the most difficult problem in P.E. because of
1)   the number of activities involved
2)   the number of children to be assessed by each teacher
3)   the time factor involved in assessing and recording.

Given that the above can be solved, the most important factor to consider is the necessity, the degree, and the standards for assessment. If P.E. counted as an examinable subject this would be obvious, but under the present circumstances how far is it necessary to go.

Some activities are more easily assessable than others, particularly those where objective standards exist, e.g. Athletics, Swimming, Gymnastics, Trampolining etc. In the majority of games activities and skills, assessment must be made in a playing situation as skill ability is of little use if it cannot be used effectively in a game also involving tactics and attitudes.

It is said that tests and measurements on the one hand contribute to better teaching by providing motivation for the pupils, and on the other hand give objective evidence which help teachers to evaluate work and make alterations which will assist in achieving objectives.

It will be to the advantage then of both teachers and pupils if as detailed as possible an assessment can be made, either by objective test (e.g. A.A.A. Five Star Award) or by teacher personal assessment. *A word of warning*—assessment should not result in a disproportionate amount of lesson time being spent on making assessments rather than on teaching physical education.

AWARDS, RECORDS, STANDARDS

A.T.C.D.E.

Abbreviation for Association of Teachers in Colleges and Departments of Education. A professional organisation which looks after the career interests of teachers and lecturers in Colleges and Departments of Education, and which is concerned in all negotiations regarding salaries, conditions of service etc. There is a P.E. section
(Secretary: S. Hewitt, B.A., A.T.C.D.E., 151 Gower Street, London W.C.1. Tel: 01.387.2442)

AUDIO-VISUAL AIDS

These can be of considerable assistance in the teaching of Physical Education in the following ways:—

1) Showing the correct methods in which skills, activities, etc. should be carried out.
2) Pointing out faults.
3) Filming an individual's performance to show where improvements can be sought—especially at higher levels of performance.

The four most common Audio-Visual Aids are:—

1) Film strips—still photographs in sequence.
2) Film loops—films of a movement or action running in a continuous loop.
3) Films—with or without sound.
4) Video-tapes—including sound.

Film Loops can be particularly useful in analysing specific movements, but it is necessary to have a projector which can advance in slow motion, or stop motion.

Films are important for analysing actions but are used more to show particular areas of activities with accompanying sound e.g. Berlin Olympics, World Cup matches, etc.

In recent years the greatest advance in Audio-Visual Aids technique has been the introduction of Video Tapes. By means of a special Video Tape Recorder, it is possible to record visual pictures from television, films, etc., onto tape, and to show these over and over again on a television set using a slow-motion technique to demonstrate actions more clearly. The current difficulty is the high cost of the Video Tape Recorder, but the system is becoming increasingly used, particularly in Colleges of Education etc. As the principle can be used in any subject the possibility of acquiring a machine in a large school is not completely remote.

In order to use Audio-Visual Aids successfully, the following points must be considered :—

1) There must be an easily accessible centre for Audio-Visual Aids to be shown.

2) The centre should be within easy reach of an area in which to practise movements just seen and analysed.

3) The Audio-Visual Aids should be competently operated to avoid waste of time or loss of sequence. This means, at very least, some practice with the particular type of apparatus beforehand, to familiarise yourself with the mode of operation and, above all, the *content* of the Aid.

4) Equipment needed should be set up beforehand so that everything is ready to operate as soon as the audience has assembled.

5) If possible, and according to situation, it is better to have an operator, in addition to the person talking about the film etc.

If these conditions are not optimum, the time taken up using Audio-Visual Aids, particularly within given lesson periods, may be out of all proportion to the advantages when compared with an actual demonstration followed by practise on the field or in the gym. The degree to which this obtains depends on how important is the analysis by the Audio-Visual Aid—the greater the quality of performance desired (high level coaching) the more importance the Audio-Visual Aids will assume.

Sportsmark Ltd. produce a chart 40" x 25" showing standard sports dimensions. This gives immediate and accurate information for all major winter and summer games ;

For details of charts write to:
                    Sportsmark Limited
                    15, Lionel Road,
                    Brentford, Middlesex.

The British Association of Organisers and Lecturers in Physical Education produce a valuable booklet giving details of films and charts for all sports.

A resume of each film is given together with information about length, gauge etc. Addresses and costs for hiring or buying of films are also included;

The booklet may be purchased from
                    Mr. L. F. Reed,
                    P.E. Organiser,
                    Education Offices,
                    Union Street West,
                    Oldham, Lancs.
                    Price 3/-

The Physical Education Association also issues a booklet on current audio-visual aids.

Various foreign Embassies and Cultural Institutes are a good source for 'inspirational' and 'documentary' films on sport and physical education.

Most sports federations also have instructional films.

AWARDS

TEACHERS. In physical education awards are mainly concerned with the coaching and refereeing of particular games and other activities and are generally to be obtained at two levels:—
1) school and club standard
2) coaching at a higher standard

Full particulars may be obtained from the Secretary of the appropriate Association (see Index).

Courses for awards are organised at various centres by local authorities and the appropriate associations in conjunction with the C.C.P.R.

PUPILS. Where awards are available they provide important motivation for improvement in individual standards. If awards are only available to expert performers, this should not lead to inadequate provision during school lessons for the majority of the pupils, but rather should be dealt with in extra-curricular activities. This particularly applies to awards of the Amateur Gymnastic Association.

The main awards available are as follows:—

Amateur Athletic Association Five-Star Awards. These are to be greatly recommended as they are obtainable by all classes of performers and it is possible for any pupil to gain an award and then improve to a higher level—from one to five star. The awards are based on individual performance in three events— 2 Field and 1 Track or 2 Track and 1 Field.

Swimming. a) *County Awards.* Each County has its own specifications for various standards to be achieved from swimming one width or 25 yards to advanced level, and including distance, speed and survival or life-saving tests. Particulars available from Education Offices or local Schools Swimming Associations.

b) *Royal Life Saving Society Awards.* Life-saving awards ranging from elementary to advanced level. Particulars available from Branch Secretary, R.L.S.S.

c) *Amateur Swimming Association.* Awards range from elementary to advanced performances in swimming and survival tests. Particulars available from Secretary, Amateur Swimming Association.

Gymnastics. Awards by Amateur Gymnastics Association based on Olympic Gymnastics to include selections from Vaulting, Agilities (Floor Work), Trampolining, Parallel Bars, Rings, Pommel Horse, High Bar. Class III to Class I, but performances for Class III above average class level usually.

Very useful motivation for Gym Club activities.

Where no awards are given by particular associations, it can be quite useful to arrange your own individual standards in various activities to provide motivation for the pupils.

STANDARDS

B.A.O.L.P.E.

Abbreviation for British Association of Organisers and Lecturers in Physical Education. Holds meetings, conferences, and courses on all aspects of the teaching and administration of physical education which are usually open to non-P.E. teachers as well. Organises a summer school.

(Secretary—D. H. Williams, Education Offices, Park Road, Hartlepool, Co. Durham. Tel. No. Hartlepool 5501)

BASIC MOTOR ACTIVITIES

The basis of all 'systems' of physical education. These are the basic activities which a human being may perform:— with his body:— e.g.

1) Walking   2) Running   3) Jumping   4) Climbing
5) Throwing   6) Swimming   7) All types of Games Skills
8) Rocking, rolling, sliding, crawling etc.
9) All other fundamental movements.

BODY BUILDING

Usually very popular with young people who are concerned with their physical appearance, especially if they tend to be thin (ectomorphic). In most instances it is attempted by weight lifting or exercising with spring and/or rubber gadgets, following courses run by various commercial concerns such as Charles Atlas, the Bullworker, etc. The disadvantage of such static exertion *on its own* is that although it is good for building individual muscles, it does not do anything for the repiratory and circulatory systems of the body, which are all important, in fitness and health. However, when combined with activities which do take these other factors into account, some form of body building is very useful to increase strength. Many training programmes followed by top class sportsmen and sports women include weight training. Probably the best type of training involving all the factors for achieving body building is Circuit Training.

TRAINING, POSTURE

BODY MOVEMENT

Two examples of body movement descriptions are provided.

Jumps. In all jumping movements there is a relaxation of the muscles of the legs with a consequent bending at the knee joint followed by a vigorous contraction of these muscles resulting in an extension of the leg or legs resulting in a thrusting of the body initially in an upwards direction combined with, or followed by, a movement forwards, backwards, or downwards according to the type of jump.

Turns. In all turning movements, one side of the body is thrust in a forwards and sideways direction using initial thrust from opposite leg or both legs assisted by an extended or partly extended arm and a movement of the head in the direction of turn with specific timing so that in a succession of turns (continuous) the head stops at the same point of each turn to obtain equilibrium and balance. There is a complementary backward and sideways thrust with the opposite side of the body. It is important that the centre of gravity should be in a vertical line with the extremities of the body to maintain balance particularly in a succession of turns.

BOOK LISTS

Several publishers issue regular book lists regarding physical education. A comprehensive guide is provided by the Physical Education Association. Teachers of physical education need to read avidly if they are to elaborate arguments solid enough to gain continuing respect for their subject.

LIBRARIES

BURSARIES

These were originally given by universities to enable students from lower income group families to study for degrees and similar awards which they would otherwise have found great difficulty in achieving because of lack of finance. As far as English universities are concerned the system of scholarships has almost died out with the institution of automatic government grants for university courses on achieving specific academic qualifications (e.g. 2 GCE "A" levels), and being accepted by a university board (governed by University and Other Awards Regulations, 1962). There are still a large number of bursaries awarded by Scottish universities.
(See publication "Grants and Awards for Higher Education" for particulars.

SPORTS BURSARIES

CALISTHENICS

Ling's system of Calisthenics is a formal way of exercising or conditioning the body. It was generally in use as a means of warm-up at the beginning of the Physical Training lesson or other physical activity. The popularity lay in the localised effect of the exercises on the different parts of the body. The popularity of this system of exercises gradually declined with the introduction of more enlightened ideas and a realisation of the wider implication of Physical Education. Present thinking suggests that warm-up exercises that approximate the skills or actual activity to be performed are more beneficial.

Nevertheless a sound repertoire of these conditioning movements, aiming at overall suppling and strengthening, are always relevant.

TRAINING

CARETAKERS

The teacher of physical education should endeavour to establish a good relationship with the caretaking staff. It is of vital importance for the health and physical education of the pupils that all the facilities are maintained in a safe and hygienic condition. Special attention should be given to all floor surfaces, particularly in the changing rooms, where verrucae are easily contracted if inadequate attention is given to cleanliness.

CARING—FOR ALL THOSE WE TEACH

Any teacher conscious of the social function of the school will endeavour to contribute to the functioning of society by equiping his pupils with the basic skills needed for living. It is in the consideration of what activities are both useful and intrinsically worthwhile that the teacher of physical education has so much to offer to the future well-being of his pupils.

Often insufficient attention is paid to the practical and creative activities and it is here that the physical education teacher can provide the necessary stimulus for exploration and appreciation. Too often it has been thought necessary to provide worthwhile activities only for the intellectual elite.

There have been many welcome changes in recent years particularly in the personal relationships between pupils and teacher. A democratic atmosphere and an integrative approach can do much to stimulate a similar response from the children. Pupils need to feel secure, to receive appreciation for their efforts, and to be able to contribute to the goals of the group. The well adjusted, sympathetic teacher has much to contribute to the development of physical, social and mental well-being of his pupils.

THE CENTRAL COUNCIL OF PHYSICAL RECREATION

The C.C.P.R. is a voluntary organisation whose function is to encourage young people and adults to *actively* take part in leisure pursuits. General Secretary is also Director of the Sports Council.

It is administered by a professional staff in London and Regional offices. It works in close co-operation with the governing bodies of sport, local education authorities, outdoor activity associations and voluntary youth organisations. In conjunction with these bodies many courses are arranged for the training of leaders and instructors and also for personal performance both at beginner and advanced level.

The C.C.P.R. maintains four National Recreation Centres— Bisham Abbey, near Marlow, Bucks; Crystal Palace, London; Lilleshall Hall, Shropshire; and Plas y Brenin, Capel Curig, North Wales. At all of these centres residential training courses are organised in co-operation with the various sports and educational organisations. At the Crystal Palace it is possible for individuals to become 'authorised users' and take advantage of the excellent facilities when not required by the centre for courses.

The C.C.P.R. provides a continuous information service for a small annual subscription, giving details of all the national and regional courses. Also included is the C.C.P.R.'s own quarterly journal, 'Sports and Recreation' which covers the whole field of sport in an interesting and informative manner. This magazine is supplied free to subscribers but can be purchased for an annual subscription of 8s.

For further details contact either your local regional office or the Headquarters at 26/29 Park, Crescent, London W.1. 01.580. 6822/9.

SPORTS COUNCIL, APPENDIX VI (S.C.P.R.)

CHALLENGE

There is no really acceptable explanation to the origin of all our needs. Amongst the many that children display is the need to achieve success. Physical Education is *unique* in the variety of challenges it provides and the opportunity it provides for success.

The teacher must endeavour to harness this inherent motivation and the following factors should be considered. First, children work hard at tasks when the result is thought to be important. Second, often when a standard of achievement has been set, greater exertion is made as long as the target is within the capacity of the child. Third, moderate competition stimulates effort.

21

It is claimed that it is the thought of the goal that stimulates the effort rather than the attainment. It creates an inner restlessness and striving.

This all suggests that Physical Education has much to offer and that the teacher should be continually confronting the child with challenging situations in which the child will be motivated to strive for a higher standard. We should be aware, however, that should the child decide to withdraw from the challenge, there may well be an inevitable loss of face in the eyes of his peers and perhaps a loss of self-esteem for the individual.

COMPETITION, VICTORY

CHARACTER

There are many meanings and much confusion about the use of the term 'character'. With regard to physical education we tend to think of 'strength of character' implying the possession of desirable moral and ethical values.

The confusion often arises because individuals who advocate particular activities, i.e. Games in the Public Schools or Outward Bound Courses, seek to strengthen and perpetuate a set of values in which they strongly believe.

There is little doubt that the participation in Physical Activities as in other areas of experience, does contribute to the development of a person's character. However, it depends to a large degree on the perception by the individual of the worth of the activity and the willingness to internalise the values.

The physical education teacher has much to contribute to the development of lasting worthwhile interests and values, but he must recognise that it is necessary to do more than just ensure participation in worthwhile activities. The desirable attitudes and values must be clearly recognisable and considered worth acquiring.

CHILDBIRTH

It was often suggested that girls who took part in active physical activities, especially sports, would have difficulty in childbirth. There is no evidence for this point of view. Athletic women show normal labour times and experience no abnormal problems with delivery. The only indication of danger seems to be heavy weightlifting which might cause pressure on the internal organs of girls.

CIRCUIT TRAINING

A considerable amount of work and research has been carried out in recent years in an endeavour to discover more efficient training methods. It is self-evident that the strength and endurance of the body can be increased by regular exercise. However, any improvement is localised to the particular muscles or organs exercised. The development of a training method which could be used to exercise all the body is of great value.

Morgan and Adamson at the University of Leeds did much to popularise Circuit Training. Circuit Training aims at the progressive development of muscular fitness, and the cardiorespiratory system. Through circuit training it is possible to cater for the fitness needs of all individuals. Initial testing is particularly necessary and the exercises should be selected to ensure that they are simple to learn, easy to perform and yet strenuous enough to provide all-round fitness for the body during the exercise session.

An exercise card should carefully record both initial testing and subsequent training scores. This enables the individual to see the results of his efforts. After a level has been reached, re-testing should take place and new targets set. Through circuit training it is possible to exercise a large group with limited or improvised equipment and still ensure quality of effort and movement. Ref: 'Circuit Training', R. E. Morgan and G. T. Adamson. Bell.

TRAINING

CLOTHING

All children should be encouraged to provide clean, comfortable, well fitting and light clothing to allow maximum freedom of movement. Where possible, after activity, showering should be the rule, with a change into clean clothing.

In cold weather it is advisable to wear a track suit when practising. The extremities should be protected.

To prevent injury, watches, brooches or any similar articles should not be worn.

If soft rubber shoes are used it is advisable to wear socks to soak up perspiration and absorb shock.

Spectacles should, where possible, be fitted with unsplinterable lenses.

DRESS

COMMITTEES

The value of problem solving groups in Physical Education has not received the attention it deserves. Valuable experience can be gained in social interaction, and in the skills of leadership. The nature of the leader has been found to influence the working of the groups to a large extent, and he can do much to ensure the members contribute and achieve a consensus of opinion. It has often proved possible to use the committee to involve an otherwise physically inadequate individual in the organisation of the school physical education programme. Such a step contributes to the individual's interest in physical activity and may also enhance his self-image.

NON-SPECIALISTS

COMPETITION

Present society is certainly competitive and one's position is gained largely through competitive skills—Intellectual, Physical or Social.

In physical education individual or team games have often been justified in the curriculum on the basis of their contribution to the competitive capacity of the participants.

Achievement and competition are two drives which are recognised by many to be inherent in our make up. However, the effect of competition on the performer is dependent on a number of factors—motivation, degree of difficulty of activity, the experience of the individual in previous competitive situations, as well as his own view of himself as a competitor. Most adults and particularly children of Junior school age derive considerable satisfaction from competitive situations and strive to do their best, but it must be recognised that for every one that experiences success many more encounter failure. It is, therefore, *undesirable* that the success of one should be contingent on the failure of another. If competition is encouraged it is necessary to develop the appropriate attitudes, and where possible link the success to more socially and educationally desirable ends, the achievement of which will provide the needed reward.

The competitive spirit should be allowed to develop normally and, where possible, channelled into co-operative activities where the interaction will serve to benefit the group and raise the overall level of performance of the group. Physical Education lends itself to group activities and every endeavour should be made to encourage co-operative attitudes and behaviour. There needs to be a balance between competition and co-operation.

CHALLENGE, VICTORY

24

CONSERVATION

Physical educationists have a special *responsibility* to encourage the conservation of nature—the conservation of an environment in which outdoor activities may take place. Full details of conservation publications and campaigns from the Countryside Commission.

CO-OPERATION

Most forms of Physical Education depend upon group co-operation. A good teacher can cultivate an understanding of the general concept of 'co-operation'

CULTURE

Culture can be viewed as a means of describing and understanding different societies. The cultural patterns can be identified by the unique education, religious, moral, economic, social and artistic institutions, expressing the basic values of the society. We can also refer to its more common use in connection with the 'cultured person' and the connotiation with the pursuit of worthwhile activities. It has been pointed out by Maheu, the Director General of UNESCO, that the roots of sport and culture spring from the use of leisure, when time and energy are freely available. However, the present social acceptance of sport has not brought forth an abundance of worthwhile cultural works. De Coubertin, who founded the Modern Olympic movement, endeavoured to integrate contests of literature, music and sculpture into the Olympic Games but these were eventually dropped, leaving only the competition and the spectacle.

The availability of leisure to the majority of the population must enable them the opportunity to appreciate and take part in cultural pursuits. It is accepted that in the participation in cultural activities the existing values will be assimilated. Therefore, the values stressed in Physical Education are of great importance, for many of our major attitudes are derived from groups with which we are associated and in which we regard ourselves as members.

Perhaps the greatest cultural attribute of sport is its ability to create beauty. Who can ever forget the Russian skaters and gymnasts or the artistry of the Hungarian footballers at their zenith.

The aesthetic value of man's physical movement must be equated with the highest level of art. Unfortunately, the fact remains that we are still without a universally acceptable movement notation and this has hampered the establishment of Physical Education as a cultural force. Without a means of faithfully recording movement it is difficult to develop traditions and aesthetic criteria for evaluating present performance and linking it with the past.

Sport and art are both capable of modifying and infinitely enriching man's experience and it is to be hoped that, eventually, sport will be recognised as one of the most worthwhile ways of developing a nation's cultural resources.

CURRICULUM—RE-EVALUATION

There is increasing support for a completely fresh look at the Physical Education curriculum. Tremendous changes have taken place in the last decade and re-organisation will cause further upheaval. The raising of the school leaving age prompts further investigation into the needs of these additional older pupils.

Considerable study and practical innovation is taking place throughout the country, but it needs to be organised and its worthwhileness evaluated. A body which has been created to undertake this is 'The Schools' Council for Curriculum and Examination'—an independent organisation formed in 1964 whose object is to promote education by carrying out research into the curriculum and teaching methods.

There is a sub-committee for Physical Education and it is at present undertaking a review of the curriculum. Teachers form a majority on the Schools Council and the result of its work is distributed in the form of reports and working papers. It also publishes a free newsletter called 'Dialogue'.

Further information can be obtained from the Information Section, Schools Council, 160, Great Portland Street, London W1N 6LL. Tel : 01.580.0352.

DANCE

There are four main factors which combine to make the dance :—

In the first place, there is the body which is the instrument and performs the movement.

Secondly, there is the intellect which discriminates and selects, thus giving the movement form and structure.

Thirdly, there is the use of the motion factors of time, weight and space which give the dance individuality, character and colour.

Fourth, there is the emotion. The emotion is the motivating force which must be experienced inwardly and controlled outwardly.

Thus the ultimate aim of Modern Dance is to make the body 'a versatile instrument capable of being used at will'.

Several individuals have evolved their own styles of modern dance ; some have withstood the test of time and are still practised today, e.g. the methods of Margaret Morris, Martha Graham, and Joss-Leeder. Perhaps the name most closely associated with Modern Dance is that of Rudolf Laban b. 1879 d. 1958. He formulated the sixteen basic movement themes each concerned with a particular aspect of bodily movement. These themes are arranged in logical progression, the first eight being elementary themes, the latter being of a more advanced nature. Due to the work of Miss Lisa Ullmann, Director of the Art of Movement Studio, the Education Authorities have accepted this Basic Classification as a sound foundation for the teaching of movement in schools.

Students are trained to teach Modern Educational Dance at all the specialist Colleges of Physical Education and at those Colleges of Education offering 'Wing' Courses in P.E.

For students wishing to qualify as specialist teachers of dance the following courses are available :—

1) A two year course at the Art of Movement Studio, Adlestone, Surrey, followed by a one year course of professional training at Trent Park College of Education, Enfield.

2) A two year course at the Dartington College of Arts, Totnes, Devon, followed by a one year course of professional training at Rolle College, Exmouth.

3) A three year course at the College of Dance and Drama, Marylebone Lane, W.1., followed by a one year professional course at Dartford College of Education, Kent.

4) The main training centre for M.E.D. is the Art of Movement Studio, a part of the Laban Art of Movement Centre. Besides the previously mentioned course for intending teachers the

Studio also offers one year courses in Movement Study and Educational Dance to trained teachers, lecturers and advisors, and also a variety of part-time courses. Full details are available from the Secretary, Art of Movement Studio, Woburn Hill, Addlestone, Surrey.

Modern Dance can also be a successful recreative activity. Personal participation and enjoyment are the first essentials, besides which it offers the experience of physical exertion, the awakening of group awareness, and the casting off of the stresses and strains of everyday living. Many recreative dance groups exist throughout the country under the auspices of the Art of Movement Guild. Full details of these classes and other courses run by the Art of Movement Guild may be obtained from the Gen. Sec. Miss Betty Osgathorp, Art of Movement Studio, Addlestone, Surrey, or from Mrs. D. M. Rickinson, 24 West Park Avenue, Kew Gardens, Surrey.

Though the actual dances have changes from time to time, Ballroom Dancing has remained one of the most popular recreations of all. For many years the accepted ballroom dances have been the Foxtrot, the Quickstep, the Waltz and the Tango, and these have been augmented from time to time by novelty dances such as the Madison and the Bossa Nova. Also popular and accepted now are the Latin American dances of the Rhumba, Samba and Paso Doble.

Many people dance regularly purely for pleasure. For those who wish to learn the art of Ballroom Dancing more seriously there are countless schools all over the country where dancing is taught both in classes and private lessons. These schools cater for both the complete beginners and also for more experienced dancers. It is a good idea to look up the names of dance teachers in the Classified Directory and choose one with qualifications who is also a member of a dance teachers' organisation. The teachers' organisations listed in the address section of this book all come under the rules of the Official Board of Ballroom Dancing. Classes in Ballroom Dancing are also held at most Evening Institutes at both elementary and advanced levels.

Although the majority of participants dance for pleasure, ballroom dancing has its competitive side, and there is a link between purely recreational dancing and competitive dancing in the system of medal tests. In these, dancers do not compete with other dancers, but simply try to achieve a certain standard. Beyond these tests there are numerous competitions, ranging from local ones to world professional and amateur championships and international matches.

Folk dancing is a much neglected aspect of physical education. It is, of course, the area of dance which, in any society, carries cultural traditions through the ages, and may have, in its beginnings, been closely linked with sport. Information can be obtained from the English Folk Song and Dance Society.

ACCOMPANISTS

DEMONSTRATION

Demonstrations can serve to illustrate good techniques, and can assist in motivating both demonstrator and the observing children. The value of teaching by demonstration can be increased when it is followed by discussion of the details and significance of the observation.

The demonstration, however, has its *limitations* and can often only be copied to the extent that the learner is able to identify himself with the demonstration and see himself in the role of the performer. Experienced teachers are often reluctant to use personal demonstrations for this reason, and prefer to use either a child or skilled verbal analysis.

It has been suggested that if the demonstration is too complex it could have a detrimental effect on the learning of a skilled movement.

Demonstrations serve their purpose if they stimulate and create the desire to improve one's own performance. Since the first time of learning is perhaps the most important 'demonstrations' when used, must be of high standard. Beware rubbish beautifully taught—an old, but vital, addage.

ABILITY

D.E.S.

Department of Education and Science. (Ministry of Education). Gives advice to teachers through Her Majesty's Inspectors (H.M.I.)

Can also give grant aid for courses, and sometimes, research. Curzon Street, London W.1. Tel: HYD 7070.

DESIGN

Two publications are of special interest and are detailed below; the journal of the I.A.K.S. (see list of organisations) is also an excellent source of information and ideas.

1. *'COMMUNITY SPORTS HALLS'*—A report of a research project by G. A. Perrin, A.R.I.B.A., DIP. TP., published by the N.P.F.A. and the C.C.P.R. price 21s.

A most comprehensive publication containing much technical information and details of interest. It is in three sections which deal with the sociological background, general planning, technical and constructional standards of Sports Halls.

2. *'BUILDING BULLITIN NO. 26'*—Published by the Department of Education and Science (H.M.S.O. 6/6 nett).

The Bulletin briefly examines the historical background to present day demands for the facilities necessary for Physical Education. There are many interesting illustrations of recommended layouts and an effort is made to relate the needs of both school and community.

DIET

The necessity for a sensible control of food intake is substantiated by many research studies. Overweight or obesity (*assumed to be 10% above the average for one's age*) shortens life, and can also contribute directly to the development of degenerative diseases e.g. coronaries. The extent to which obesity has been shown to cut down life expectancy is startling. Moderate overweight produces a 40% higher than usual risk, making obesity a 70% higher death rate for one's age. No long term reduction in weight can be achieved without a change in eating habits.

Obesity also reduces the amount of activity that a person is prepared to undertake and if dieting is to be effective it must be related to activity levels. Studies have indicated that there is a definite advantage in reducing weight by a combination of dieting and exercise. The suggestion that increased activity will increase the intake of food is not borne out by studies:— It has been shown that moderate exercise of short duration does not step up food intake.

The commencement of obesity in adults has often been found to relate to a reduction in physical activity while at the same time the appetite did not decrease. This indicates that the diet must be controlled together with as much exercise as possible to give the best possible foundation for physical well-being.

The normal adult, by means of a reasonable variety of foods, is provided with sufficient essential vitamins to keep the body weight at an optimum level.

Proper nourishment is essential in the early years if the foundation is to be laid for future health and well-being. Particularly as children grow their need for more food becomes apparent, and, as adolescence is a period rapid growth, the need for a well balanced diet is vital.

There is a considerable problem with regard to the dissemination of information about the constitution of a well balanced diet particularly as it is essential that individuals should appreciate the function of foods. A wise choice can then be made to ensure sufficient supplies for body building, regulation and protection, and fuel.

'Overweight' must be seen in relation to the three basic body types—ectomorphy (thin), endomorphy (fat), and mesomorphy (muscular).

DISCIPLINE

The aim of every teacher of physical education should be to motivate the children to identify themselves with his concern for the worthwhileness of physical education. The use of coercive techniques are of little value and usually serve only to alienate the pupils from the subject.

The teacher should use his position as an authority and his enthusiasm for this branch of education to create intrinsic interest in physical activity. He must endeavour to equip his pupils with the skills necessary to question what he is doing in a knowledgeable way. *'The teacher is an agent of change as well as challenge'.*

Obviously in physical education it is necessary to maintain order to ensure everyone's safety and in this there is the tendency to become authoritarian. In the games situation or in the swimming pool, commands are necessary for rapid and unambiguous direction, but should only be used when really necessary. self-discipline should be the aim.

Nevertheless even the most capable and inspiring teacher is occasionally confronted with pupils whose attitudes or behaviour are unacceptable. On these occasions it may be necessary to impose conditions of order to enable the learning to proceed.

The form of the punishment will depend very much on the nature of the offence and should be in conformity with the established school practices. In other words the teacher will be able to select from a number of alternatives available to him the most suitable for the occasion.

The experienced teacher will endeavour to anticipate and avoid situations that create disorder and thus avoid the necessity of resorting to punishment. Good teaching still requires the ability of the teacher to obtain regular discipline. Untidy dress, slovenly habits of movement, and a poorly organised pattern of activities in a lesson cannot lead to really useful learning.

DISCUSSION

The questioning technique can be used to profit in modern physical education, but can be overdone. Sit down 'q' and 'a' sessions can never substitute for activity. Remember that questions should more often than not be answered by movement.

DRESS

'Dress' *is* important for both teachers and children. The teacher must set standards. Dress should be appropriate for the game or activity. High standards in dress are important both for aesthetic reasons and also as part of the effort to cultivate a 'group' as opposed to an 'individual' outlook. Concern with dress should imply also concern with cleanliness. Smart dress need not be expensive—any school could have small 'slips' made for little expense—these could be worn for all indoor activities and could be laundered collectively on a regular basis. Dress can also be used to educate a love for colour—(*why only white ?*).

APPENDIX V, KIT, CLOTHING

DRUGS

"IT IS GENERALLY RECOGNISED THAT THERE IS NO KNOWN MEDICAMENT WHICH GIVES RISE TO AN IMPROVED PHYSICAL PERFORMANCE WITHOUT AT THE SAME TIME PRODUCING HARMFUL SIDE-EFFECTS."

The taking of artificial stimulants by Athletes, in an endeavour to improve performance, is a serious problem and one that is viewed with grave concern by the governing bodies of sport.

Although the problem is not a new one and not especially relevant to the school, the knowledge of the effects of doping should be made known to all pupils. Teachers should remember that tobacco and alcohol are both drugs.

The Council of Europe formed a special working party to consider the situation and formulated a clear policy statement—for further details see reference. They condemned the taking of drugs on Legal, Moral, Social and Medical grounds. They felt that it was a 'Dangerous form of moral deception' and socially, the need to achieve good results should not lead to the health, or future, of young athletes being harmed. On medical grounds the value of drugs in raising the standard of physical performance is very doubtful. The main dangers being :

    a) the elimination of the natural warning reaction of fatigue, which could result in extreme over exertion.

    b) the disturbance of the natural co-ordinations of the physiological and psychological functions of the body.

    c) abuse, habit formation and possible addiction.

ref : Doping of Athletes,
    Report of the Special Working Party, Council of Europe, Strasbourg, March 1963.

EDUCATION

The Educational process is life-long and all-embracing, it is therefore not confined to school age or school time.

Education today suffers from the sad dichotomy of having an educational theory which is essentially sound, but which is difficult to put into practice because of the examination system imposed upon it. The long term effects of this dichotomy would appear to emphasise a series of dualisms between the value of examined and non-examined subjects, and between the intellectual and the physical. Symptoms like these indicate a lack of harmony in education. Until such time as a major overhaul comes about, the prime responsibility for balance and synthesis must remain in the hands of the individual teacher. Since a teacher of an examined subject is largely the slave of his syllabus, the real opportunity must lie with teachers of non-examined subjects. Here the *physical educationist* can help to rectify the imbalance and lack of synthesis.

EFFORT

1) Although it is important to improve physical function through a knowledge of correct movements and a well-educated nervous system, conscious effort is needed in order to succeed in competition. Best results come through knowing just when and with what strength to impose the will on the body, to produce greater effort without a breakdown in co-ordination.

2) The work of Rudolph Laban showed that in man's efforts, whether functional or expressive, whether in work or in recreation, whether in large movements of the whole body or small unconscious movements of parts, there can be found common factors and principles.

See "Effort" by R. Laban, written in collaboration with F. C. Lawrence (Macdonald & Evans Limited). A handbook of Modern Educational Dance by Valerie Preston-Dunlop.

ENDURANCE

Endurance is necessary in order to maintain work of a high quality without performance being affected by fatigue. It is in two parts; first, an efficient heart and lung mechanism to ensure general stamina; second, muscular endurance which enables muscles to reproduce identical movement without tiring. These basic physical requirements are acquired through coaching, training and conditioning.

ENERGY

Metabolism is a term employed to embrace all the chemical processes carried on within the cells of the body. One of these processes is the oxidation of food materials with the production of energy. Heat is a form of energy, and all other forms of energy, such as mechanical energy, electrical and chemical energy can be reduced to heat. By measuring the heat produced by a fuel when it is completely burned, the total amount of energy which the fuel contains can be ascertained. It thus becomes possible to express food energy in terms of heat. In physiological heat measurements, a calorie is the quantity of heat required to raise the temperature of 1 kilogram of water one degree centigrade.

Estimates of the energy expenditure during various activities are useful for; computing dietary requirements; assessing the severity of activities; and for determining optimum means and rates of work. Considerations of human performance in work and sport usually involve some combination of these three.

ENJOYMENT

Enjoyment is an important and legitimate end of every aspect of physical education. To *strain* after enjoyment is to limit the interpretation of this happy state to fun and hilarity. It should, therefore, not be uncontrolled on the part of the child, nor obtained at the expense of the teacher. (At all ages intense interest may be sober, taking the guise of serious concentration).

True enjoyment results from the satisfaction of an innate hunger for the mastery of skills, and the attainment of self-expression through these skills.

EQUIPMENT

Fixed and portable apparatus for use indoors or out, should be of suitable design and construction with emphasis on strength, stability and good finish. Portable or movable apparatus should be safely stowed when not required for use. Arrangements must be made for *regular* inspection and adequate maintenance by knowledgable persons. Damaged apparatus should not be used.

Great care is needed in the choice and use of portable equipment. The activity equipment such as bats, sticks, balls and rackets should be suited in size, weight and design to the age, strength and ability of the players, should be of good quality, and should be in a state of good repair. Plimsolls are suitable on hard surfaces but appropriate studs or spikes will be necessary for many activities on grass.

APPENDIX V

EVALUATION

Evaluate your work systematically and regularly. Don't press on regardless—you *could* be wrong. Evaluate each lesson—ask yourself—did I teach something ? Did the children learn something ? Did we all enjoy it ?

EVENING INSTITUTES

Evening Institute work, apart from being worthy in itself, is a useful way of supplementing income. A class of 12 is usually required—and a space. Direct contact with the Institute concerned is the best way to get things going. Many Local Education Authorities require teachers to possess specialist coaching awards issued by national governing bodies (see Appendix).

FACILITIES

Detailed information on all the sports facilities in a region can be obtained from each of the 9 Regional Sports Councils in England and Wales. R.S.C. lists differentiate between public and privately owned facilities. Owners or managers of privately owned facilities frequently welcome bookings from schools, especially during normal school hours as these are usually their least busy times.

The Local Education Authority Physical Education Advisers are usually helpful in finding some additional facilities for schools whose own facilities are inadequate.

Teachers who are involved in planning future facilities for their schools should refer to Regional Sports Councils to check whether other, similar facilities are being planned nearby. For technical information on matters such as building specifications, flooring, lighting, court-making, etc., refer to "Community Sports Halls" by G. Perrin (N.P.F.A. and C.C.P.R., 1965).

SPORTS CENTRES

FAIR PLAY

Nothing is more damaging to physical education than reports of disputed decisions, fighting, biased refereeing, and other aspects of unfair play. The physical education teacher must accept responsibility for the behaviour of his pupils in all areas of competitive sport, and the emphasis must be on obedience to the letter and spirit of the laws of the game. Provocation, however extreme, can never be accepted as an excuse for unfair conduct. Courbertin Fairplay Awards are given annually by UNESCO for outstanding examples of sportsmanship.

VICTORY

FARTLEK

Fartlek is a Swedish word meaning 'speed-play' and the fartlek system of training gives a runner a lot of training over distances far greater than his competitive distances. Each training session should last for 1-2 hours and should be repeated 3 to 5 times a week. A typical fartlek training session could include:

1. 10-15 minutes jogging or easy running.
2. 1 mile run at fast, steady speed.
3. 5 minutes rapid walk.
4. 10 minutes jog with 5 sprints of 75-100 yards.
5. Spring uphill for 150-200 yards.
6. Jog 1 mile with frequent 5-10 yard bursts.
7. 10 minutes rapid walk.
8. 1-5 laps fast running, depending on competitive distance.

This can be varied according to the runner's level of fitness, the distance for which he is training, and the time in the season. Fartlek training offers more variety than most training methods, and can be continued throughout the year. It is particularly valuable for middle distance runners.

TRAINING

FEET

Proper care of the feet is essential. Neglect can result in fungus infections and in athletes foot. Feet should be washed frequently, dried thoroughly, and powdered. Toe-nails should be cut straight across, not rounded, to prevent the risk of in-growing toe-nails. Hypertrophied toe-nails (horny, thickened, yellowish or blackish in colour) should be treated by soaking them in a solution of bicarbonate of soda and carefully filing them.

Cushion in-soles of foam rubber or cork are cheap to buy and can be worn inside gym-shoes. They can be changed and washed at frequent intervals. In-growing toe-nails *must* be inspected by a doctor and pupils should be dissuaded from home operations.

Floors of gymnasia and changing rooms should be sprayed daily with a disinfectant solution.

Barefoot work in the gymnasium is excellent: barefoot running on grass is also recommended at the end of a training session.

VERRUCAE

FEMININITY

The suggestion that taking part in sports makes girls 'masculine' is false. Naturally, girls who have narrow hips, broad shoulders, and are muscular—like boys of the same physique status—do well at sports. This is not to say that the sports cause these! Sports provide millions of girls and women with opportunities for healthy exercise and self expression. The biggest girl can find creative satisfaction in training for sports; 'better fit than fat' might be the appropriate maxim. The best girls are often better than good men. Girls have brought to physical education and sport, a certain grace and rhythm, and have enriched both the work and themselves.

MENSTRUATION

FINANCE

The amount of money available to the physical education department from official sources is normally decided at least 12 months in advance, after consultation between the Headmaster and the Head of Physical Education. Distinction must be made between Capital Equipment (identifiable items additional to equipment already on inventory) and Revenue Equipment (identifiable item replacing equipment already on inventory.) An allowance may also be made for hire of additional sports facilities. The inflexibility of such financial sources means that most physical education teachers rely to some extent on unofficial sources of finance. These include:

1. *SCHOOL FUND.* Usually controlled by the headmaster and financed by weekly contributions from pupils plus profits from school social functions.

2. *SALE OF SPORTS CLOTHING.* Either via local retailers who pay the school a small commission on all sales, or through mail-order firms (such as Darlows of Sheffield). The latter method may be cheaper to pupils, but can be very time-consuming. Some school secretaries will help.

3. *PUPIL CONTRIBUTIONS.* Pupils taking part in lunch-time and evening sports activities can be asked to pay a small subscription, either each week or each term. This often encourages them to take the activity more seriously. Older secondary school pupils who expect a wide range of physical education options can be asked to pay part of the cost of the more expensive activities.

4. *SUPPORT FROM LOCAL FIRMS.* Some firms will agree to sponsor a school team for a fixed annual amount, or will buy sets of team shirts. (This needs tact and discretion).

5. *PARENT-TEACHER ASSOCIATION.* Potentially the source of a great deal of money, goodwill, and direct labour for

the construction of swimming pools, climbing walls, adventure courses, etc.

Teachers who have access to money from one or more of these 'unofficial' sources should ensure that they keep an accurate account of all income and expenditure, and that the account is readily available for inspection and audit.

FIRST AID

In addition to the first aid kit which is kept in every gymnasium, sports hall, or playing field, physical education teachers should carry a first aid field kit to all sports activities. This kit should contain small quantities of all the items in the main first aid kit, and should include a copy of a first aid booklet, together with a separate accident report book.

ACCIDENTS, SAFETY

FITNESS

Fitness for what? The beneficial effects of regular exercise may be summarised as follows:
1. Muscles develop and muscle tone improves.
2. Appetite is stimulated.
3. Respiration is stimulated and deepened.
4. The lymph and blood circulation are quickened.
5. Because of improved circulation waste products are cleared more rapidly
6. General metabolism is improved: a feeling of well-being results.

A more detailed exposition of the advantages of keeping fit can be found in the introduction to "Physical Fitness" (Penguin Book 2055, 1965). Adult interest in the subject can be stimulated by a controversial book such as "Be Fit or Be Damned" by Percy Cerutty. (Pelham Books, 1967, 30/-)

JOGGING, TRAINING

FUN

More than any other part of the school curriculum, physical education should be fun. If an activity makes those who participate miserable then, whatever its theoretical value, it should be modified or abandoned. When the physical education teacher evaluates a lesson his first question should always be *"Did the pupils enjoy it?"*

ENJOYMENT

GROUNDSMEN

Our happiness depends on them. Remember the value of friendship and the occasional present. Endeavour to implant in the pupils a satisfactory attitude towards the 'Groundsman'.

GROUPS

Children are helped to develop more understanding and tolerance of one another by working in groups. The nature, functions and properties of groups, hold great significance for the teacher of physical education. Groups in sport are usually less than 24 and fit into a sociologist's definition of a 'small group'.

Ways of changing groups round in a gym can be stimulating; a different class will demand 'Cross leg sitting in straight lines' perhaps; an average group can be handled with less formality; a good group might be self-organised or take its leads from instruction cards issued prior to the lesson proper.

It is worth reading chapter 6—"Education and Physical Education" by J. Myrtle James (G. Bell & Sons Limited).

TRANSFER

GROWTH AND DEVELOPMENT

The Developmental point of view within psychology suggests that present behaviour can often best be understood if we know something of its history, for the child is indeed "father of the man". The human infant, like other animals, is born with a wide range of possible behaviour. His maturation depends upon his physiological growth potential and the characteristics of his species. He becomes an individual through his experiences as he grows up—experiences in interacting with both the physical and the social environment.

The process of socialisation—the training for group living given by the cultural environment in which an individual happens to be born—has much to do with adult behaviour.

ADOLESCENCE

GYMNASTICS

Various forms of gymnastics are in vogue. Gymnastics of any kind are set apart from other sports and games because they—

1. Set out for 'good' movements as an aim, not a by-product.
2. Often form a good basis for condition training for all other physical activities.
3. Provide a greater range of movement than any other single activity.

Gymnastics needs good teaching; don't neglect gymnastics teaching because of its specialised demands.

The teaching of educational gymnastics does not demand the ability of an acrobat. All teachers can handle educational gymnastics, but a good knowledge of anatomy and physiology is still *essential* if the 'right' movement questions are to be put to the children for 'movement solutions'.

HANDICAPPED

This can infer a variety of factors which may be physical, mental, emotional or social in nature. Included under the classification of physical deviation are postural deviation, heart malfunction, nutritional difficulties, locomotive problems, speech impediments, vision and hearing defects. Emotional deviations may include those of mental retardation and the many emotional maladjustments such as aggressiveness, anti-social behaviour, withdrawal or depression. The mentally handicapped child could be a genius or one who is mentally retarded. Socially, handicapped children could include those who have specific deviations in their human relations with others.

The physical educationist should endeavour to meet the needs of the children who fall into this category. The handicapped child must be helped to accept himself, and to find ways in which he may substitute activities and gain satisfaction from these substitutions.

HARVARD STEP TESTS

Any worthwhile training programme should contain a schedule for regular measurement of the various factors that make up training and conditioning. Logically, the best efficiency test of the heart and lungs is the actual measurement of the amount of oxygen the body can absorb per minute. Such a procedure involves the use of rather elaborate apparatus.

A simpler method is to use changes in the pulse rate with exertion. The Harvard Step Test was devised in the Harvard University Fatigue Laboratories and measures the heart-rate recovery after exercise. The person performing the test steps on and off a bench twenty inches high, thirty times in one minute. The test continues to a maximum period of five minutes. When the exercise is completed the athlete sits, while his pulse rate is taken and recorded. For full details see "An Introduction to Tests and Measurement in Physical Education" by W. R. Campbell and N. M. Tucker (Bell & Sons Limited).

TRAINING

HEALTH EDUCATION

The physical educationist is still looked upon as a resource for information on health information. In games, teachers get to know children intimately and can often give invaluable help on health matters, especially those which are unusually embarrassing and concern personal hygiene and sex. If, for example, when young boys are distressed or accutely embarrassed by physiological manifestations in the changing rooms, the physical education teacher by the carefully chosen word can alleviate the distress or ridicule.

Health should involve not only the efficient functioning of the body machine, but playing one's part in the full richness of living. The World Health Organisation defines health as *"A state of complete physical, mental and social well-being, and not merely the absence of disease and infirmity."*

Since Physical Education is to do with the mind as well as the body, the question of health is a subject of real importance. The two-way process of the mind affecting the body, and the body affecting the mind, does indicate that the state of the organism is an important aspect of health. By keeping the bodily organs in a fit and functional state, there is less likelihood of them distracting the mind from its work.

Organic fitness may be regarded as an integral part of total health and it is the responsibility of the physical educationist to administer and promote a programme that will bring it about.

APPENDIX IV

42

HEALTH EDUCATION COURSES

A number of courses exist for training in health education—a useful 'second string' for the physical educationist. Courses in Health Education are run by the University of Birmingham and by the University of London. The Health Education Council can give information about these. The Royal Society of Health offers correspondence courses. In London University, Health Education is now part of the Academic Diploma in Education, and the B. Ed. degree, as well as being a Diploma course in its own right. The Health Education Council runs an Annual Summer School in Health Education.

HOBBIES

Remember that many hobbies can be based on sports and could be *"exploited"* more cleverly by physical education teachers. Collecting news pictures and statistics about sports and sports people is a common hobby—often lifelong—for millions of people. One finds songs based on football supporters' groups and motifs concerning sports clubs. The connection between sports and other hobby areas is open-ended.

ALL PEOPLE

IDEAS

Be productive with ideas. Keep abreast ; never give up thinking. Renew 20% of your programme every year and every five years you will have a totally new approach. Don't be afraid to learn from other teachers—and from the children. Children have more fertile minds than teachers.

INCOME TAX

PROFESSIONAL ASSOCIATIONS. Teachers may qualify for relief under Section 16 Finance Act 1958, in respect of Professional Association subscriptions. They will be allowable as a deduction from his emoluments assessable to Income Tax—Schedule E. Claims should be made on forms P.358 obtainable from your Local Tax Office.

P.E.A.

CLOTHING AND LAUNDRY. The P.E.A. undertook lengthy negotiations, on behalf of its members, with the Board of Inland Revenue to obtain the following concession :—

'To the allowance of a reasonable deduction for the cost, in so far as borne by the teachers, of the renewal of gymnastic uniform and personal games equipment required for the purpose of performing his or her employment'. Such an allowance is only granted on expenses 'wholly necessarily and exclusively' incurred in teaching duties.

In making claims teachers are advised to prove expenditure. It is up to the Local Tax Commissioner to allow any particular expenses. Claims may be made retrospectively, up to six years.

The P.E.A. has prepared an information sheet for the guidance of its members.

INFORMATION

Useful information, especially regarding addresses of sports organisations in sport, can be obtained from the Information Service of the C.C.P.R., 26 Park Crescent, London W.1. Tel: No. 01.580.6822

LIBRARIES, P.E.A.

IN-SERVICE TRAINING

The C.C.P.R., LEA's and the National Governing Bodies of most Sports hold frequent courses for teachers who wish to coach a particular activity at school. Your Regional C.C.P.R. office will provide you with a list of courses in your area, or will be able to put you in touch with a body which is likely to be organising a course in your particular interest.

The following are known to provide short/vacation courses in Physical Education, Sport and Recreational Activities specifically for teachers. Blackpool Easter School, Winchester Summer School, Loughborough Summer School.

PART-TIME COURSES. Most Universities offer Part-Time Certificate or Diploma Courses for serving teachers. In many of these it is possible to offer Physical Education as part of the course. A list of courses is available—"A List of Higher Degrees in Education" from The Secretary, A.T.C.D.E., 151 Gower Street, London W.C.1. (1/6d. including postage).

FULL-TIME COURSES. The Department of Education and Science has approved arrangements whereby serving teachers may be seconded for one year, in order to study for a 'Higher Qualification'. Full conditions, and details of such courses, may be obtained from the booklet "A Programme of One Year Short Courses", published annually by the Department.

L.E.A'S

INSURANCE

The teacher of Physical Education has a number of special considerations concerning insurance. (See also section on Legality). Most L.E.A.s have their own Insurance Cover for Schools and Teachers in their service, teachers are advised to contact their Education Office and find out 'exactly' what this cover involves. The P.E. Specialist is advised to check especially cover concerning :—

1. Transport of Students in Staff Cars.
2. Personal Accident.
3. Third Party Claim.
4. Coaching. It is as well to remember that whilst you may enjoy Insurance cover as a teacher employed by a school or L.E.A., this cover will not extend to private coaching.

The P.E.A. offer comprehensive insurance cover, for members for a relatively small premium.

P.E.A.

INTEGRATED STUDIES

Physical education can be the basis from which integrated studies can be launched—it needs little imagination to lead from sport to sculpture, painting, literature, international relations, race relations, law, ethics, architecture, and field studies etc. World sport is an international nonlingual language. Always remember this unique aspect of P.E. work.

INTERNATIONAL SPORTS FEDERATIONS

Almost every sport has its own international federation. The first, for gymnastics, was established as early as 1881. ISF's regulate rules for their sports throughout the world. Addresses of all international sports federations can be found in the Yearbook of the Union of International Organisations—usually available in a good reference library—or can be obtained from the Reference Section of the C.C.P.R.

45

INTER-SCHOOL ACTIVITIES

Inter-School Sporting activities are one of the very few 'links' between schools, at pupil level, and as such have an *important* social aspect which should not be ignored. Without sports how else could schools communicate on a mass basis and at child level?

Much of your time will be spent arranging Inter-School activities. Experience suggests that the following should be borne in mind when arranging a fixture list.

1. Make all fixtures well in advance. (At least one term ahead is necessary if you intend to publish a 'Fixture Calendar').
2. All fixtures should be made and acknowledged in writing; this avoids misunderstandings over the telephone. The 'phone may be used for emergencies and final rain checks.
3. Do not be too ambitious. A saturated fixture list reduces the efficiency and enjoyment of teams and staff.
4. It is as well to have a 'Distribution List' for regular information —particularly for last minute arrangements and alterations— this should include:—
   a) Coach Company
   b) Team Manager—Team
   c) Groundsman
   d) Headmaster
   e) Refreshments 'bodies'.
5. Extend competitions on a *broad base.* Do not concentrate only on the elite. Why not several teams playing in inter-school matches?

INTERVAL TRAINING

This is a formal, disciplined, fast-slow training schedule performed over measured distances. The athlete/swimmer works to a plan and sets himself to run over a number of 'fast' sectors at specified time speeds, interspersed by fixed 'slow' recovery periods. The claim is that Interval Training cultivates speed and endurance at one and the same time. It is endurance training at approximately racing speed. Planning an Interval Schedule will depend upon:—

1. The length of the fast intervals.
2. The number of fast intervals.
3. The speed of the fast intervals.
4. The length/duration of the recovery intervals.

TRAINING

INVOLVEMENT

The success of any Physical Education programme depends upon the involvement:

a) *OF PUPILS*

b) *OF OTHER MEMBERS OF STAFF*

PUPILS INVOLVEMENT IN LESSONS
Maximum activity, minimum teacher's 'chat'.
Introduce variety—don't work on same task too long.
Allow students to work at their own level.
Be enthusiastic (even if they are the worse group in the school).

PUPILS INVOLVEMENT IN EXTRA CURRICULUM ACTIVITIES
Good publicity—Notice Boards, Announcements etc.
Knowledge of Results—keep competitions, league tables etc. up to date.
Encourage senior pupils to help as Officials.

INVOLVEMENT OF STAFF
The success of your programme depends not only on fully involving your pupils. Variety and depth will depend upon your ability to involve as many other members of Staff as possible to assist as coaches, team managers, referees, or in any capacity which will release you to deal with some other aspect of the programme. One way of involving staff may be to encourage them to use the facilities of the P.E. Dept., in their own time for their own enjoyment (Staff Badminton or Tennis etc.) Public relations is a very important aspect of Physical Education if you are going to achieve staff involvement.

AIMS

IOC

The International Olympic Committee has its headquarters in Lausanne. Established in 1894 by Baron Pierre de Courbertin, the first IOC contained seven teachers out of fifteen members. Courbertin saw sport, education, and international understanding as the three pillars of the Olympic movement. The IOC is a self-electing group responsible for the management of the Olympic Games and the spread of 'Olympism'. Its structure was modelled on that of the Roman Catholic Church and of the Knights of Malta. It is still the most powerful force in world competitive sport.

ISOMETRIC TRAINING

An Isometric muscular contraction is one in which the muscle remains the same length, because it is opposed by a resistance which cannot be overcome. It is a static contraction. Professor E. A. Muller found that for a given muscle or muscle group, a single daily isometric contraction of six seconds duration, at $\frac{2}{3}$ maximum effort, produced rapid strength increases.

Pressing the palm of one hand against the other is a simple and individual illustration of isometric training. An all-body isometric programme can be worked out by commonsense.

Isometric Training should be left alone unless you are prepared to study it seriously. *There are possible dangers,* which must be fully understood prior to application.

TRAINING

JOGGING

"Jogging" is a term for simple walking/running routines which can help delay an early coronary. The idea of "Jogging" has swept New Zealand and the U.S.A. in recent years. The whole family can take up "Jogging".

ALL PEOPLE

JUMPING

In all kinds of jumping the quality of the jump and landing is more important than the variety. A clear distinction should be made between 'yielding' landings where the body gradually absorbs the energy of the jump, and 'resilient' landings where the landing is immediately followed by another jumping movement (as in skip-jumping).

The teacher who wishes to coach athletics jumping events effectively, must have an understanding of the laws of mechanics. These are explained clearly and concisely in "The Mechanics of Athletics" by Geoffrey Dyson (U.L.P. 1968 (4th Ed.) 35/-).

Jumping is specific—you must teach jumping for basketball, for volleyball, for gymnastics, and for athletics, etc.

KEEP FIT

How to *keep fit* is still probably the most important question to the layman and one which the physical educationist should be able to solve—for all shapes and sizes.

More and more people try to avoid heart troubles by taking regular exercise. P.E. teachers should move out of the school and into the community to give better leadership in this fitness area.

The Keep Fit Association can help women teachers start Classes.

The Medau Movement Society can help similarly as can the Ladies League of Health and Beauty. Men could also try to start general fitness classes as part of Evening Institute, or Sports Centre, work.

ALL PEOPLE, JOGGING

KIT

Kit need not always be in short supply. If it is, someone (Headmaster or Education Officer) is not working efficiently in your cause. If you ask every child in your class to bring along one tennis ball or one plastic ball you will probably find a 100% return. Try it !

APPENDIX V

LABAN

Rudolf von Laban was one of several Europeans who developed movement theories between the wars, (Bode, Medau and Loges are others). Laban worked in this country and his influences in dance movement education, and educational gymnastics are now ubiquitous. His theories are based on the neat categorisation of movement into the four basic elements of weight, space, time and flow. There are several texts on Laban's movement theories and many Colleges of Education now base their work on 'Laban'.

LAUGH

What has happened to the *fun* in physical education ? One sees not enough smiling, not enough happiness, among teachers of physical education. To laugh—both the teacher and the taught —from time to time—is not a sin !

FUN

LEA'S

Local Education Authorities usually run in-service courses and employ advisers, organisers, or inspectors to help teachers with their work. Make a special point of getting to know the officials of the L.E.A. whose fields of activity and interest impinge upon Physical Education. Take every advantage of the possibilities which exist to improve and update your knowledge.

Some L.E.A.'s are introducing lengthened half terms so that teachers can be brought together for 'Up-Dating'.

IN-SERVICE TRAINING

LEGALITY

It is in connection with accidents to children and students that most teachers and organisers will be concerned legally. Accidents do happen, not infrequently, though few are of a serious nature.

The basic point is that when a child is sent to school, the parent surrenders for the time being part of his exclusive right to direct and control the child. This delegation of power to a school-master or club leader is often expressed by stating that the master is "in loco parentis". This means that for his particular purpose the master has the same obligations, and the same rights and duties, in relation to the child, as its own parent, but only so far as is necessary for the welfare of the child.

1. The teacher must act as a wise parent, therefore if medical aid seems necessary it should be summoned immediately.

2. Accidents should be immediately reported to the Local Authority or Governing Body.
   Reference "Some aspects of the Law relating to Physical Education Teachers" from the Physical Education Association.

If a student on schools practice is your responsibility *remember* that you are at all times legally responsible for his work.

ACCIDENTS, STUDENT SUPERVISION

LESSON NOTES

Even for practising teachers of long experience, lesson notes—no matter how short—are essential.

PREPARATION

LIBRARIES—COUNTY

Under the Dewey Decimal Classification system, most County Libraries hold most of their stock of books in one particular field in one or two libraries. Thus, one library may hold a large stock of books on Computers while another branch holds a large stock on Ancient Chinese Art. Within your County one or perhaps two branches will hold a relatively large stock on Sport and Physical Education. The library lending system usually produces any book you require in a short time.

LIBRARIES—SCHOOL

The Physical Educationist's duties are not entirely in the Physical domain. It is to be hoped that his work will stimulate the young people in his charge to a wider interest in the cultural aspects of Sport and Physical Education. This aspect of the work can best be achieved by ensuring that the school has ample and up-to-date literature on all aspects of the subject, both in the school library and perhaps in the games area (changing rooms) where a small library of magazines, articles etc. can be kept for reference at odd moments.

LIBRARIES-SPECIALIST

Apart from the Libraries of Colleges of Education and University, the P.E.A., at Ling House, provides the only known 'Specialist' Library in the country, which, together with an extensive information service is open to members of the Association.

P.E.A.

LIVENERS

A good teacher should have a number of activities up his sleeve for 'livening up' lessons. Such games as *'O'GRADY SAYS'* and *'CRUSTS AND CRUMBS'* still have a use—build up a repertoire of these activities to throw into your teaching. You will be surprised how effective they can be. Remember—we can all bore our classes from time to time.

MATTING

Matting, rubber or other material, down the sides of the gymnasium or sports hall, allows spectators in freely without recourse to the 'take off your shoes' philosophy. Spectators are part of the game and should be welcomed.

MEDICINE

Sports Medicine is a neglected field. The British Association of Sport and Medicine and the Ergonomics Research Society are two British organisations interested in the subject. There is a definite need for physical education teachers and doctors to come closer together.

International work in sports medicine is organised by F.I.M.S., and I.C.S.P.E. (see Unesco). F.I.M.S. (the International Federation of Sports Medicine) is recognised by the World Health Organisation and by the International Olympic Committee.

HEALTH, APPENDIX IV

MENSTRUATION AND PHYSICAL ACTIVITY

There are differences of opinion regarding the effect of menstruation on athletic performance. There is evidence that some changes in the menstrual cycle may result from the physical and mental stress associated with athletic activity, but they are usually slight and of short duration.

Harik claims that women, during menstruation, will not be harmed by the most strenuous activity, and that all normal actions should be continued (note the continued performance of dancers, ballerinas and acrobats).

Karpovich reported studies that indicated that a woman's strength decreased a few days before the menstrual period. He suggested that ultimately it is a matter of individual assessment, because it also is necessary to take into account other anatomical, physiological, sociological and aesthetic considerations on an individual basis.

If any unusual changes are noted to occur periodically in association with physical activity it is suggested that the individual should be referred to her local doctor for a medical report.

Harnik, M., Sport and Menstruation, Manila: Bureau of Printing, 1955.

Karpovich, P. V. Physiology of Muscular Activity, W. B. Saunders Company 1953.

FEMININITY

METRICATION

Physical education and sport will be a useful way of encouraging an understanding of metric measurement. This will be particularly so with regard to court measurements etc.

MINI SPORTS

Adapted forms of sports are widening the scope of the activities and making them available to more people at varying standards. Mini-basket, Mini-volley, and 'Five a side Soccer' have become recognised activities. (In Africa the International Basketball Federation uses Mini-basket to introduce the game). Write to the sports federations concerned for information.

MOTIVATION

Several studies have shown that no one motivation is, in itself, adequate for a group. Motivations vary from *'to meet other people'*, and *'to get away from the house'*—among adults—to *'to please teacher'* and *'to get stronger'* among children. Different 'motivating techniques' should be used concurrently to catch the largest number. Sometimes narrow programmes taught well, leaving a 'hunger for movement as part of a balanced life', are as useful as wide programmes containing touches of various leisure time skills. Remember that boys as well as girls like to have nice figures and attractive movement patterns—although they rarely admit it.

ZEST

MOVEMENT

Movement has become a much used, sometimes misused, term in physical education. In some cases it has become the 'umbrella' term to embrace what has previously been known as recreation, physical education, etc. etc. Whatever terms the teacher uses to classify the different elements in the work he should not become a slave to them. As physical education teachers, however, it is necessary to be aware of, and interested in, current attempts to formulate ideas and classify material concerning 'movement studies'.

LABAN

MUSIC

Music is a much neglected aspect of physical education programme. As a background to weight training and circuit training, as rhythm for calisthenics, and as an ingredient in dance.

ACCOMPANIST

NATIONAL COASTAL RESCUE TRAINING CENTRE

A centre, started in 1969, to teach surfing, sea canoeing, sailing, and many forms of sea rescue.

Afan Lido, Aberavon, Wales. Tel: Port Talbot 4141

NATIONAL OLYMPIC COMMITTEES

All countries have a National Olympic Committee responsible for controlling the entry of teams in Olympic Games. Sometimes these NOCs are virtually Ministries of Sport (as with C.O.N.I. in Italy) ; often they are responsible for the development of both Olympic and non-Olympic sports (as in many developing countries) ; in Britain the Committee is mainly devoted to fund raising. In 1968 many NOCs decided to form themselves into an 'international group'—the Permanent General Assembly of National Olympic Committees, with a Secretariat in Rome.

From 1970, the British Olympic Association will collaborate in efforts to support the International Olympic Academy in Greece. Here an annual summer school is held on matters concerning Olympism and physical education. Scholarships offering free board and half travel are available.

Inf. British Olympic Association, 12 Buckingham Street, London W.C.2.

I.O.C.

NEWTON'S LAWS

The analysis of movements cannot be undertaken unless you know the simple mechanics of motion. Athletics events, diving, gymnastics, can only be taught well by those who understand the principles of levers, rotation etc.

NON-SPECIALISTS

The physical education programme in all primary schools and many secondary schools depends on the enthusiastic support of the non specialists. As 'specialist' you must always be aware of the need to cultivate friendly relations with interested members of staff. The modern 'specialist' needs to act as an 'organiser' of the human material available to him. Draw in to your programme all possible help—there is on record a school where the caretaker runs the cycling club !

COMMITTEES

NOTATION

Several forms of notating movements have been invented. The most well known are Labanotation and Benesh Notation. Special courses are also run by Valerie Preston-Dunlop, at the Beechmont Movement Studios, Sevenoaks, Kent.

LABAN

NOTICE BOARDS

The good department, in many schools, can be recognized from the school corridor wall newspaper. Cuttings from the press, photographs, statistics etc., can be arranged in a stimulating fashion—very often by the children themselves.

OBESITY

One of the most important causes of *early death*. Obese people die before their time. Exercise does help to counteract the tendency to put on weight—especially if dietary care is also taken.

HEALTH EDUCATION, WALKING, DIET

ORGANISERS

Organisers and Inspectors are able to offer valuable advice and services. Teachers, organisers, lecturers, sports managers, recreation officers, etc., are all part of a team. Don't hesitate to ask your organizer to call on your school and keep an eye open for the many in-service refresher courses which are organised throughout the country.

L.E.A's.

OUTDOOR ACTIVITIES

No physical educationist can be unaware of the importance of outdoor activities such as canoeing, sailing, climbing, walking, camping, orienteering, etc. Activity on water and under-water are further areas under this classification.

One cannot be an expert in all areas but a special effort should be made to attain proficiency in at least one outdoor activity, and a general understanding of activities which 'take man in close communion with nature'. Such activities are also useful in teaching children of the importance of conservation.
Information:

"Outdoors" published by the Physical Education Association.

The Countryside Commission (European Conservation Year) 19 Belgrave Square, London S.W.1.

Many Outdoor Activity Centres are now in operation. Most LEA's now have such centres which can be used by schools.
YOUTH HOSTELLING, ALL PEOPLE, HOBBIES, APPENDIX VI

OUTINGS

Sports visits can be invaluable in developing both fairplay and good spectator behaviour. Such values must be taught; they cannot be left to chance. Winning graciously, losing gracefully, etc., are important values resulting from well taught watching as well as playing.

Visits to Lords Cricket Museum (where Real Tennis may be seen) and to good films on sport, are other possible 'outings'. For rural children a visit to an urban sports centre like the Crystal Palace is also an 'outing' of note; for city children a day by the river is similarly stimulating.

TRAVEL

OVERLOAD

The principle of overload is basic to all forms of resistance-condition training. The organism must work at full pressure in order to respond effectively.

TRAINING

PARENT TEACHER ASSOCIATION

Much more co-operation between PE Departments and PTA's could take place. Particularly in primary schools this could be enormously helpful.

PHYSICAL

The first component of 'physical education'. Whatever else we do, we must take care of the 'physical' in man. People want and need trim physiques, efficient circulatory and muscular systems.

AIMS

THE PHYSICAL EDUCATION ASSOCIATION OF GREAT BRITAIN AND NORTHERN IRELAND

The Association is a non-Governmental body. Founded as the Ling Physical Education Association in 1899, it exists to encourage and facilitate the scientific study of the physical health of the community through physical and health education, through recreation, and through the methods and practices thereof.

ITS OBJECTS MAY BE FURTHER BRIEFLY SUMMARIZED AS FOLLOWS
1) To educate and instruct specialist teachers, in physical and health education and recreation, in current theory and practice both in the United Kingdom and Overseas and the best methods of improving the physical health of the community.
2) To facilitate the exchange of information, knowledge, and thought on these subjects, and maintain means of information thereon.
3) To encourage the formation of branches, societies and committees throughout Great Britain.

THE PRINCIPAL WAYS IN WHICH THE ASSOCIATION FUL- FILS THESE OBJECTS—ARE:
a) *research* by individual authorities or by groups of experts
b) *publications* embodying these and other researches
c) *meetings and discussions* addressed by leading authorities
d) *an information and advisory service* which supplies facts and answers to problems

e) *a reference library* including a comprehensive collection of relevant British and foreign periodicals
f) *a lecture service* which supplies speakers on all aspects of physical and health education and recreation
g) *a book department* which stocks and supplies publications on these subjects.

MEMBERSHIP

Membership is open to suitably qualified or interested candidates, who must be nominated by two members known personally to them. Applications should be made to the General Secretary. The membership of the Association shall consist of:

a) Ordinary Members, who shall be men and women who—
   1) were ordinary members of the incorporated body immediately before the incorporation of the Association ; or
   2) hold a degree of a British University or a teaching diploma or certificate recognised by the Department of Education and Science, The Scottish Education Department, or the Ministry of Education for Northern Ireland, and are actively engaged in teaching some aspect of Physical Education, Health Education or Physical Recreation or
   3) hold a senior or advanced coaching award of one of the Governing Bodies of Sport or
   4) Hold another equivalent professional qualification in Physical Education, Health Education or Physical Recreation.
b) Associate Members, who shall be men and women who—
   are interested in the aims and work of the Association.
c) Overseas Members, who shall be men and women who—
   have obtained, in a country outside the United Kingdom, a certificate or diploma qualifying in the view of the Government of the country concerned to serve as full-time teachers of Physical Education, Health Education or Physical Recreation.
d) Student Members, who shall be—
   men and women who are engaged on a course in Physical Education, Health Education or Physical Recreation which would qualify them for Ordinary Membership.

SOME SPECIAL FACILITIES THROUGH MEMBERSHIP

The British Journal of Physical Education (bi-monthly) including Research Section, Abstracts, International Affairs, Students' Dialogue, Book Reviews, Around the Colleges, News from the Affiliated Societies.

Appointments Register: Members requiring posts are advised weekly of whole-time, part-time and emergency vacancies.

Library Members have the use of a lending library from which books can be borrowed on all aspects of physical and health education and allied subjects. For the convenience of those unable to visit Ling House, the Association's Headquarters, a postal service is available. There is also a separate Reading Room. Photocopying can be arranged.

Ling Book Shop Books covering all branches of physical and health education, including games, may be purchased from the Associations' Headquarters. A full list will be sent on application.

Information and Advisory Service It is at the disposal of Members free of charge, and from time to time it issues special notes, such as "Some Aspects of the Law Relating to Physical Education Teachers", and "A Guide to the Assessment of Fees for Part-time Teaching".

Courses and Conferences Events arranged by the Association are normally open to Members.

Legal Liability and Aid Insurance A special cover can be arranged for an annual premium of 3s. against Members legal liability arising out of accidents occurring during activities, both in and out of school hours. The indemnity thus provided is up to £50,000 for any one accident.

Personal Accident Insurance Compensation will be payable in the event of the death or disablement of a member as the result of an accident whilst carrying out the duties of his or her appointment. The protection will extend not only to accidents actually happening during schools hours but also during extraneous duties voluntarily undertaken in the member's capacity of School Teacher. Members may choose one of two alternative Schemes. Annual premiums of 3s., or 15s., each year according to benefits.

Income Tax Subscription to the Association may be set off against Income Tax liability.
Further particulars can be obtained on application.

SUBSCRIPTIONS DUE ON JANUARY 1st EACH YEAR, THE ANNUAL SUBSCRIPTION IS AS FOLLOWS:

	£		
1) Ordinary, Associated, or Overseas Members Resident in the United Kingdom	3	3	0

2)	Ordinary, Overseas Members			
	resident abroad	3	3	0
3)	Retired Members	1	10	0
4)	Joint Members (Husband & Wife)	4	4	0
5)	Student Members (for academic			
	year)		15	0
6)	Corporate Members (basic)	5	5	0
	Corporate Members (full)	15	15	0

New Members, other than those just leaving college, joining after July 1st may pay half the subscription to cover Membership only until the end of the current year. Those recently qualified may pay 15s. on joining and need then to subscribe only £2. 8s. on January 1st, following.

INQUIRIES

All inquiries, enclosing a stamped addressed envelope, should be addressed to the General Secretary, The Physical Education Association of Great Britain and Northern Ireland, Ling House, 10 Nottingham Place, London W1M 4AX Tel: 01.486.1301-2

All teachers should support this national professional association.

PLAY

Various theories of play, explaining its relaxing, its recreating, its rejuvenating, and its channeling of excess energy, benefits have been enunciated. From time to time remember them, or study them. Play should pervade physical education at all levels. Ref: Sport in Society, P. MacIntosh Watts.

POSTURE AND PHYSIQUE

Postural education was a valuable baby which went out with the 'Ling bath water', a grave mistake. 'Adaptive physical education' is not for a small fringe group, but for everyman. All teachers of physical education should understand the relationship between tension and posture, and other similar relationships. Physique grading and personality differences should also be understood.

Teachers should be keenly aware that boys, as well as girls, desire a 'trim' figure.

POTTED SPORTS

Make sure you have a 'potted sports' circuit up your sleeve. (Simple potato races, picking up matchboxes, etc.). Make a standby plan and keep it for a rainy day, or for when two or three classes are joined together because of staff absence.

WET WEATHER

PRIMARY PHYSICAL EDUCATION

The Plowden Report contains a long section on physical education in primary schools. It recommends that children should be exposed to gymnastics, swimming, running, jumping and throwing, outdoor activities, games and dances throughout their education in primary schools.

PRE-COLLEGE ADVICE

Teachers should take care in advising children on a choice of colleges. Apart from listed courses of a well known nature, many other colleges offer 'main' courses which can lead to B.Ed. degrees. Write to the ATCDE for detailed information.

PREPARATION

All teachers must prepare every individual lesson throughout their whole career, even if this preparation lasts only a minute before the lesson and the 'notes' are mental! Before each lesson the teacher should reflect—"*I must teach something—the children must learn something*".

PRESSURE TRAINING

A basic training system much used in games training. It consists of deliberately creating intensive methods of skill practice which are much *harder* than those required in the game itself. An enjoyable and purposeful method, highly recommended.

TRAINING

PROBATIONARY YEAR

The first year of teaching should be looked upon as still a year of *study*; a chance to develop an individual technique from a generalised training. In-service courses, the advice of experienced teachers, and the guidance of organisers, should be welcomed (and willingly given without patronage).

IN-SERVICE COURSES

PROBLEM APPROACH

The 'problem approach' in education gymnastics, (e.g. here is an obstacle—get over it in three different ways) demands a knowledge of physiology and anatomy if it is to be really well taught. A back-ground biological understanding enables teachers to ask the right movement questions for the individual physique to answer.

PULSE

Apart from accelerating the pulse rate by enjoyable purposeful activity—keep your finger on the 'pulse of the lesson'.

PUTTING

For 6th form groups the local putting green can be a happy, if occasional, diversion for the whole group !

OUTINGS

QUALIFICATIONS

Apart from initial teaching qualifications the additional qualifications which can be gained can be divided into two main categories.

1. ACADEMIC

B.ED. DEGREE. For those who have not already obtained this degree it is possible to take courses that lead to the degree providing that initial qualifications were obtained through a three year course. Very little has been done to provide part-time in-service courses but Lancaster University has already started and it is hoped that other universities will announce their plans shortly.

DIPLOMA IN EDUCATION. This award can be gained by following a one year full-time or two year part-time course at most universities.

M.ED. or M.A. DEGREE IN EDUCATION. The regulations vary but usually an Advanced Diploma is required as a necessary qualification.

Details of the latter two awards will be found in the booklet published annually by the Department of Education and Science entitled 'Programme of one year and one term courses for Teachers'. This is distributed to all schools. The A.T.C.O.E. also publish a booklet on Higher Education courses (see A.T.C.O.E.).

DANCE. A one-year course for qualified teachers at the Art of Movement Centre.

OPEN UNIVERSITY. Full details obtainable from Chris Batten, Admissions, The Open University, P.O. Box 48, Bletchley, Bucks.

2. SPORTS COACHING ETC.

Details can be obtained from the sports bodies listed in the appendix. Courses to prepare for awards are often organised by the C.C.P.R. and enquiries should also be made with them.

VACATION COURSES, AGEING

QUALITY

Be careful not to get involved in providing such a wide range of activities that the quality of the teaching, or quality of pupil performance, deteriorates. It is far better to provide a narrow range of activities well within the capabilities of pupil, teacher and facilities.

In teaching, always strive for quality of movement even in the simplest skill. It seems fashionable to disregard standards in the name of freedom to create individual skills, this is a *gross error*. Remember that every movement has a beginning, a middle and an end. There are starting positions and finishing positions. Sometimes straight lines, straight backs, and immediate reaction to instructions, together with good posture and pointed toes, are valid teaching points. Don't use modern methods as an excuse for lazy teaching.

SKILL LEARNING

QUEST FOR TRUTH

Every teacher should strive to remain open-minded regarding theories in physical education. There is too much either/or thinking in our work and not enough either/and. There should be a constant search for truth, throughout ones career.

RECORDS

Record cards for individual pupils can give useful references to school careers. Cards should contain such information as date of birth, home address, school group or house, class, any known disabilities, school teams played for, sports awards gained (e.g. A.S.A. personal survival). Particular aptitudes or interests should also be recorded.

REPORTS

RELATIONSHIPS

The three most important good relationships for a physical education teacher to cultivate are :—
1. With other members of the school staff
2. With school sports organisations both locally and nationally.
3. With local sports clubs and associations
All these people have a vital part to play in the work of the physical education teacher. Without their co-operation the work of the teacher will be severely restricted.

PARENT TEACHER ASSOCIATION, NON SPECIALIST, COMMITTEES

RELAXATION

An important phase of exercise. In order to get the full benefit from exercise one must teach pupils to relax *properly* during and afterwards. It is possible to achieve a state of relaxation through the practice of specialised exercises. Another way is through hydrotherapy.

During skilled movements the ability to relax unneeded muscles makes for smoothness and delays the onset of fatigue. Relaxation should not be confused with idleness, but associated with leisure and recreation. We have learnt a great deal about switching people 'on' for high performance—not enough about techniques for switching them 'off'.

YOGA, TRAINING

REMEDIALS

A much neglected aspect of physical education in schools and colleges. The need can be illustrated by the fact that, in a recent survey, nearly sixty per cent of physical education students at a college were found to have fairly serious postural defects. As many teachers are not adequately educated in this field, courses to correct this deficiency should be demanded or sought.

Almost everyone requires 'remedial' physical education.

POSTURE

REPORTS

End of term reports can be a nuisance, but it must be remembered that they are designed to give parents a guide to progress. 'Good', does not tell them much about progress. Try to make constructive comments on the work, or alternatively pick out only part of the work that deserves comment. Record cards can be useful aids in compiling reports.

RECORDS

RESEARCH

For information on the results of recent research the Physical Education Association should be consulted. If you are undertaking research it is also advisable to consult the P.E.A. for access to the extensive catalogues of abstracts, books, etc.

Research should be practical as well as abstract, joint as well as individual.

Don't be put off by research 'mumbo jumbo'; research in sport can be fascinating.

RUNNING

A basic movement which is an enjoyable exercise when carried for its own sake. Running can be done in various ways to provide variety.

TRAINING

SAFETY

Some sports have particularly hazardous elements, e.g. mountain activities, canoeing, sailing. *No* teacher should teach these skills without careful training. Neck holds in judo, wrestling involving throwing, and other combat sports must be treated with great care. Games like rugby must be played strictly according to the spirit of the laws or they are lethal activities. Boxing is the only sport in which one is allowed to inflict brain concussion within the law of the activity. Many teachers believe that boxing is not a suitable activity. The Royal College of Physicians have published a study on injuries in boxing which should be studied; although this study was on professional boxers we should bear in mind the remarks of an eminent neurologist in the House of Lords (Lord Brain), who said, "The brain cannot distinguish between an amateur and a professional blow !".
Take special care with cycling.

ACCIDENTS

65

SCHOOLS COUNCIL

The Schools Council has a physical education committee which would always be glad to hear from teachers with interesting suggestions on curriculum reform and other matters.
Schools Council—160 Great Portland Street, London W1N 6LL

SKILL LEARNING

The successful acquisition of physical skill is extremely important to the teacher of physical education.

Very often in achieving physical skill the action of big muscle groups is most readily acknowledged, but fine motor co-ordinations are often necessary too.

Basically there are two major methods of learning skills—the brick by brick approach (progressive practices), and the whole-part-whole approach. The former is used in diving for example; the latter in squash.

Skills lessons are opportunities for quality *learning* and *teaching*. A typical lesson's plan might run—rehearsal of known skill in a perhaps more advanced situation than previously; introduction of new skill; game situation; game. (Challenge introduced where the teacher thinks appropriate.)

The difference between closed and open skills should be understood.

CLOSED SKILL

In this type of skill the technique is of primary importance. The person learning a skill builds up a pattern of movement which is as closely aligned as possible to the theoretical best. He must of course take into account his own physical make up. In building up a successful pattern of movement the sportsman ignores all external influence, concentrating only on the perfect execution of a skill. This skill can be thought of as the building up of a number of habits to meet predictable requirements; it is typical of many athletic events, e.g. javelin, shot putting, or diving and vaulting.

OPEN SKILLS

These are skills where other factors than techniques are important. Environmental factors have to be specifically taken into account.

In the competitive game situation the player must not only have good technique but he must be able to use this at the appropriate time and in the most successful manner. It is insight, or being able to read the game, which is of greatest importance here, and being able to adapt to varying situations.

The circumstances in which an 'open' skill is performed are likely to be highly unpredictable, and rarely repeatable. The successful soccer or hockey player is the one who has mastered the techniques of the game and can then translate these techniques into the ever changing pattern of competition.

SPECIAL RESPONSIBILITY ALLOWANCES

These are common; it is up to you to *fight* for an allowance. Often allowances for 'P.E.' are halved to accommodate the 'boys' and 'girls' requirements. Contest this arrangement; where Departments are separated they should be treated separately with regard to allowances. There are growing opportunities for special responsibilities in primary schools.

SPORTS BURSARIES

Sports Bursaries are now being awarded to young potential Olympic sportsmen.

Applicants for this Government sponsored scheme should be between 15-18 years of age, and must be either in full time education, or employment, or in an apprenticeship.

The bursaries offered are a maximum of £500 a year. The awards will be supplemented by local authority grants and parental contribution.

The C.C.P.R. or the Sports Council can give full details.

SPORTS CENTRES

Sports Centres have developed rapidly in the last few years. Harlow was one of the first; now all new towns have Sports Centres.

Sports Centres built or approved since 1966.

NORTH Workington, Thornaby, Billingham Forum, Eston, Wallsend, Ponteland, Newcastle, Durham, Stockton on Tees.

NORTH WEST Birkenhead

YORKSHIRE AND HUMBERSIDE Rotherham, Kingston on Hull, Huddersfield, Sheffield, Gainsborough, Keighley.

WEST MIDLANDS Warley, Stoke on Trent, Tipton, West Bromwich, Walsall, Stratford (pending result of enquiry), Madeley.

EAST Peterborough

GREATER LONDON AND SOUTH EAST Crystal Palace, Guildford, Folkestone, Lee Valley, Newham.

SOUTH Bicester, Basingstoke, Easthampstead, Stoke Manderville, Basildon, Bracknell

SOUTH WEST Poole, Plymouth, Brockwell, Bishops Clevel

WALES Cardiff, Port Talbot, Harwarden, Wrexham, Aberdare, Harlech

SCOTLAND Glasgow (Bellahouston), Perth, Aberdeen, Glenrothes, Edinburgh (Meadowbank), Cumbernauld.

Sports Centre and Recreation management is a 'new' profession for the physical educationist.

SPORTS COUNCIL

Established in 1965 as the Government Advisory body on all sports matters. Chaired by the Minister responsible for sport; technical 'servicing' is provided by the CCPR. Sports Council, 26 Park Crescent, London W.1.

Seeks to link government, local authorities, and governing bodies of sport. It is an advisory body having no executive powers. It endeavours to advise Government on matters relating to amateur sport and physical recreation. It also grants aid to organisations, clubs, and, occasionally, individuals.

SPORTS DAY

A booklet on how to organise an Athletics Meeting can be obtained from the Amateur Athletics Association.

STANDARDS

In Athletics, the "Five Star Award Scheme" has revolutionised the teaching of the sport. Standards have been calculated for all events.

All sports can provide standards and simple achievement tests. Survival Swimming Awards are a further example.

AWARDS

STOP WATCHES

Stop watches should be run and wound *regularly.*

STUDENT SUPERVISION

Physical education students on school practice will need varying degrees of help, bullying, cajoling, protecting and restraining. *You have a moral and a LEGAL responsibility.*

HELP them by selecting reasonable classes. Give them as wide a variety of work as possible. Suggest some positive scheme of work to be covered during the period of the practice.

BULLY them into being punctual if necessary, make sure their schemes of work, lessons plans and observations are adequate, accurate and up-to-date.

CAJOLE them into coming back to help with Sports Day, Swimming Galas and helping with Saturday morning matches.

PROTECT them from their supervisors. If it is a first practice shelter them from the worst of the discipline problems.

RESTRAIN them from doing too much and becoming exhausted. Stop them from becoming too familiar with the children. Keep a careful ear open for their language.

DON'T use them as cheap labour.

REMEMBER when they are working with apparatus, a fully qualified member of staff must be present to assume full responsibility.

CHECK on their swimming qualifications, make sure they have some life saving award.

SUBSCRIPTIONS—IN

There is much to be said for small subscriptions, from children and from parents, to funds for promoting extra activities or purchasing special equipment. Imaginative fund raising schemes can be great fun for all concerned. Sometimes the 'sub' can be in kind, (e.g. 'one tennis ball per child' can make starting tennis much more enjoyable).

SUBSCRIPTIONS—OUT

Subscriptions to recognised unions or professional associations may be set against tax. These would include N.U.T., N.A.S., A.A.M., P.E.A. Tax relief can't be gained unless you pay your dues to the association first !

P.E.A.

SWIMMING GALA

Advice on the organisation of a Swimming Gala can be obtained from the Amateur Swimming Association (A.S.A.)

TALENT

Talent is an individual's special aptitude for a specific function or range of functions. It can be manifested in numerous ways and the extent to which it is inherent in the individual, or created by circumstances, is a matter of debate.

Physical talent can be functional, expressive or athletic for any of the wide field of physical activities. It can be expressed in team games, or in individual performance (that is, dancing, track events etc.), and it can appear in a variety of settings.

There is argument about how an individual is endowed with talent—as to whether it is physiological or psychological. The most likely answer is that it is made up from both, and also much influenced by home and environmental factors. The perceptive teacher should be constantly watching to see the exact areas for which a child is most suited by his own physical character, and equally by his own natural predisposition and inclination. No-one can predict exactly when talent will be manifested or when a change of circumstances will reveal it. Tests and measurement can be used but the results should not be regarded as necessarily permanent.

ZEST

TEAMWORK

The real word should be co-operation, which implies abandoning individualistic ideas and voluntarily agreeing for the sake of the group to collaborate, integrate, and work together for the side. In any team game, the individual can be both sublimated and submerged all within five seconds or five minutes. All must work for all, all must work for each, and each must work for all, and each must work for each.

GROUPS

TELEVISION

A part of the lives of most people in Great Britain but called by different names according to one's class or mood. Commonly blamed for violence, social unrest, crime, sexual promiscuity, juvenile delinquency, and bad harvests. Most serious academic critics would support the view of Professor Himmelweit (Television and the Child) that television cannot instil values but can in some cases reinforce them. (See too J. D. Halloran!—The Effects of Mass Communication). Like the internal combustion engine, television can be used for good : the spread of knowledge and information, or bad : mass consumption of mindless trivia. The teacher should endeavour to teach children to criticise television—to discuss not just the good programmes, but also the bad, so that children become aware of serious criticism Encourage children and students to watch all programmes concerning physical and movement education and to analyse their content. Ask them to consider the amount of time allocated to specific sports, how it is dealt with and why.

Use programmes to start discussions and as starting points for consideration.

TERMINOLOGY

Science of symbols and signs which must be *correctly* used in the study of the movements of human bodies. These signs can be used for artistic or scientific accuracy and by their very detailed and microscopical graphics the accuracy of their representations will be conveyed to the reader. All terminologies have to be learned and in physical education, or the study of movement, attempts range from shortening of the (A/S) English Language (rather like Latinisms) to the symbolic shapes and signs of the Benesh and Laban notation systems. For any terminology to be successful as a wide communicating system it must be universally learnt and known. At present, as with chemical signs and formulae, terminology for movement is understood by a small percentage of people. Every teacher develops his or her own private terminology—a useful safeguard if one's log book is mislaid.

TESTS

Tests can be used in many shapes and forms and at all times of the year, and can be adapted and changed for all ages and sexes and aptitudes and motivations. There is no area in which a teacher cannot create a test, it need not necessarily be athletic or aquatic, it can be an expressive or artistic field.

The most important point to remember about tests is to assess continually their rightness and their value to the individual and the class. There are many books on tests and measurements, but no teacher should use these rigidly and apply without care and thought.

STANDARDS

TIME

Time is the mode by which we perceive the succession of events and the phenomenon of change; to a physicist there is no absolute time, but for a down-to-earth teacher the portion of time allotted for teaching, or to a specific purpose, is probably the most absolute point in time. A child in growing, develops a concept of time through an awareness of the rate at which his own movements proceed—the extremes of slow or fast. Time is developed through a union with length and distance so that longer distances, or more meandering ones, are compared with short straight passages from A to B. The formal teacher of grammar believes time is learnt through past, present and future tenses; a scientist feels time is learnt by looking at the Bristol (Clifton) Suspension Bridge and seeing the gorge below; and the music teacher believes time is learnt as in mathematics by rhythm, number and emphasis, and duration. The teacher of physical education can use time mathematically, scientifically, biologically, musically, artistically, in fact in any analogical way, provided he studies all the pages written on *TIME* in the Oxford dictionary.

TIMETABLES

In primary, secondary or higher education timetables are a bug bear to the P.E. Teacher. Allocation of time as for art, or domestic science subjects, often means that children have all their gross neuro-motor and physical social activity on one day of the week. Variety and a daily lesson are better than a weekly two hours. Try to have *summit* talks with the headmaster or the time-table maker, and put the point of the value of functional, expressive, athletic and aquatic etc. work, being woven into a week's time-table.

PAGES 113, 114, 115

TRAINING

A period of discipline for a specific objective: all children should train in one respect or another—for an examination, for a test or a display.

Points to remember are:—
1) Boredom is the first enemy of successful training.
2) Self-training is by far the most worth-while.
3) Training human beings is not the same as training animals; an altogether different system of reward and encouragement needs to be used.

BODY BUILDING, CALISTHENICS, CIRCUIT, FARTLEK, HARVARD STEP TESTS, INTERVAL, ISOMETRIC, OVERLOAD, PRESSURE, RELAXATION, WEIGHT

TRANSFER

This is what a physical education teacher knows how and when to do, in the manipulation of teams, or even in class and gymnasium problems. Removing, shifting, conveying a person from one spot or place to another, altering impressions, or/and attitudes, and/or opinions, can all occur because an imaginative teacher can anticipate cause and effect. As if solving a continually evolving jig-saw puzzle, a teacher of games studies skills and aptitudes, and transfers when either time, or space, or dynamics, or flow, are needing a boost. Transfer, in skills learning, occurs best where the possibility to transfer is pointed out by the teacher, it is not automatic and could be *negative.* Values might be transferred if the teacher tries hard to explain the similarities in situations.

TRAVEL

A very worthwhile part of the school curriculum, which can involve the teacher in a school journey overseas, or merely an afternoon at another school. For the children it will inevitably be an exciting time because of the break in routine and change of environment. Whatever the circumstances, organisation is inevitable, vital and essential. Certain points should be remembered:

1) Staff—the number of staff should be adequate to cover staff or pupil illness.
2) Information—everyone should be told how, when, where and why they are going; the pupils should not merely be regarded as so many sheep to herd about.

OUTINGS

UNESCO

Purpose, *"to contribute to peace and security by promoting collaboration among nations, through Education, Science and Culture, to further universal respect for justice, for rule of law and for human rights and fundamental freedoms which are affirmed for people without distinction of race, sex, language or religion"*.

In 1960, The International Council of Sport and Physical Education was set up under the auspices of UNESCO as a world forum of sport and physical education. It now has 140 members including 19 international sports and physical education organisations.

UNESCO is interested in sport from its educational and social role. As the scientific nature of physical education increases the need for international co-operation increases. It also has a significant contribution to make to mass culture.

UNESCO has become more active in sport and physical education. The International Council of Sport and Physical Education (ICSPE) has published a Declaration on Sport, and several other documents of the same nature. ICSPE has also initiated Courbertin Fairplay Awards which are awarded annually at UNESCO House, Paris. ICSPE co-ordinates research and documentation. Membership is at international, national, non-governmental, governmental and individual levels.

ICSPE also works closely with the International Council of Health, Physical Education and Recreation (ICHPER), and the International Federation of Sports Medicine (FIMS). ICSPE has committees for sport and sociology, leisure, tourism, history, work, development, etc. Addresses of these and other international physical education organisations are to be found in the Appendix.

Individuals can join several of these organisations. To be international in outlook is more rewarding than to be insular. A comparative assessment of a situation can be more enriching.

"The Declaration on Sport" is a document costing 2 NF which sets out clearly a modern philosophy for sport. It is available from ICSPE at UNESCO House, Paris.
Address: 7/9 Place de Fontenoy, Paris 7E, France.

UPWARD JUMP

The simple test of vertical jumping ability is a sure test of power. Sometimes called the Sargent jump. Marked boards to measure this jump are sold by Sportsmark—see audio-visual aids.

VACATION COURSES

There are many vacation courses. The most comprehensive for the physical education teacher are probably:
    1. Loughborough Summer School.
    2. B.A.O.L.P.E. Summer School.
    3. N.W.C.P.E.A. Blackpool Easter School.

Information regarding these and many other courses are to be found in the Times Educational Supplement, the journal of the Physical Education Association and the information sheets published by the various local authorities.

Expenses for attending these courses can usually be partly met by application to the L.E.A. but, as schemes vary, further information on the matter should be obtained from the Local Education Office.

QUALIFICATIONS

VARIETY

It is as important to maintain variety in the physical education programme as it is anywhere else. A never ending diet of soccer and cricket, no matter how popular they may seem to be, is of no real benefit to boys (hockey and rounders for girls) and will soon become boring to the majority. In addition such a practice would be educationally unsound.

On the other hand beware of the opposite extreme. Facilities, and personal ability, will limit the width of programme that can be undertaken while still maintaining standards. Anything wider will produce jacks of all trades and masters of none.

VERRUCA

Children's feet should be checked regularly for indications of this infection. They can usually be identified as a hard, painful, dark coloured type of wart on the sole of the foot. Medical treatment should be sought. They should not be neglected.

The infection can spread rapidly so adequate precautions must be taken if it is detected.

No work in bare feet should be permitted by children suffering from verruccas. On no account should they be allowed to go swimming.

A useful disinfectant for dealing with verrucca and preventing further outbreaks is VANODINE, supplied by W. C. Evans, & Co. Ltd., Eccles, Manchester.

FEET

VICTORY

An *important* factor in sport, much *underrated* in Britain until recently. As a teacher, one must be careful of two extremes when coaching children.

a)   Playing down the importance of winning to the extent that both the morale and the motivation for playing the game are put to a low ebb.

b)   Winning at all costs, even to the extent of teaching the rather underhand that one may have picked up in one's previous playing experience.

One should also pay as much attention to the *problems* of being a 'loser' or a 'permanent loser'. Being a good loser does not always satisfy injured pride or lost face.

CHALLENGE, VICTORY

VOCABULARY OF MOVEMENT

A very useful aid to teaching. If labels can be attached to various basic movements, then the teaching of more advanced skills using a combination of these can be greatly enhanced. Unfortunately no one has yet devised a universally accepted notation method.

LABAN

VOICE

The use of the voice is far more effective than a whistle in the control of a class engaged in physical activity. In the gymnasium, which is usually badly designed accoustically, particular attention should be paid to voice control in order that all pupils can hear instructions clearly. The best result can be achieved by altering the pitch of the voice rather than increasing the volume. A loud voice in conditions of echo can be more difficult to follow than a whisper.

In open spaces, trying to convey instructions of more than one syllable can be particularly grating on the ear, to say nothing of the throat of the speaker.

Instructions can be seen in three parts—explanation/pause/expletive. It is the third part which conveys the mood of the movement—e.g. "To the far end of the gym", (quietly and carefully)—pause (for the message to sink in)—"Run!!" (with vigour or calmness as the case may be).

WALKING

The basis of all physical conditioning programmes. Every training programme must be based on regular walking. Walking is perhaps the best 'sport for all' activity and the neglect of it could be a major cause of obesity, etc. The best effect from walking is gained when it becomes 'effort', orientated, i.e. a deliberate attempt is made to walk quickly, strolling along is better than nothing but not good enough. If people walked upstairs instead of taking elevators, and walked two tube-stations distance to work, they would be fitter and feel better.

OBESITY

WEIGHT TRAINING

There are several good books on weight training. In a nutshell there are two main forms.

Muscular endurance—i.e. small loads lifted a number of times.
e.g.   20 lbs. 15 times rest/again/rest/again.

Power—i.e. increasing loads with decreasing repetitions, e.g.—

                    100 lbs. five times
                    120 lbs. four times
                    130 lbs. three times
                    140 lbs. two times
                    155 lbs. once

Special *safety precautions* must be taken. Keep the back straight and use the legs, keep the weights near the midline of the body, keep the feet about shoulder width apart. Don't *play* with weight training ; if you are not sure, go on a course.

TRAINING

WET WEATHER ALTERNATIVES

Always have films, competitions, visual aids, and other 'tricks' up your sleeve for a wet day. Wet weather periods provide P.E. teachers with a chance to talk to children about health education, fairplay, leisure and recreation, and other intellectual aspects of the work.

POTTED SPORTS

WINTER SPORTS

Winter sports have grown rapidly in this country. They provide physical education teachers with a golden opportunity to display organisational powers and to introduce children to one of the most exhilarating sports known to man. Winter sports expeditions tie in nicely with 'integrated studies' involving geography, international relations, history, etc.

A number of Travel Companies make special provision for schools groups and provide free places for party organisers.

OUTINGS, TRAVEL

X-COUNTRY

Cross country running is still the basis of British middle distance running. Foreign coaches say they envy our 'running culture'. Beware of overdoing it, especially for the fat, unfit, and unwilling,

X-KEEPING FINGERS CROSSED

A disease commonly diagnosed amongst teachers at end-of-term displays, exams and all other occasions when their fitness to teach the young is about to be judged. Variants on the disease (in its chronic stages) include crossing the toes, knitting of the brows, general tenseness of the body and an inability to speak in anything but high pitched titters. Prolonged suffering from the disease should be avoided, as otherwise a permanently glazed expression will result, with severe cramp and nausea as other common symptoms.

X-RAYS

X-rays are penetrating radiations, which although invisible to the eye can affect suitably prepared photographic film and luminescent screens. The study of X-rays has had a profound influence on the history of physics, particularly knowledge of radiation and the atomic structure. X-rays are probably generated naturally in the interior of hot stars. On earth they are usually obtained by means of X-ray tubes which must be ray-proof and shock proof.

X-rays have many industrial applications—searching out flaws in materials and checking processes, observing decay in old paintings and verifying genuine old masters. Even in the customs sheds—X-rays have uses.

In medicine and particularly in sports medicine their use is invaluable for all fractures, sprains and dislocations. In general education mass radiography for chest and polluted air disorders and for detecting the common gastro-intestinal disturbances, is available to all. Blood with all its constituents can be tracked through the kidneys and the heart, and the focus of malfunction thus traced. From being used to study pathological processes X-rays can now be used to study normal structure, growth and exercise and the whole respiratory and metabolic peristaltic process. This is invaluable for all training purposes allied to humidity, height above sea level, and temperature variables.

The physical education teacher should be conversant with the X-ray department of the local hospital for practical and down-to-earth reasons.

X-UNKNOWN FACTORS

These can be briefly summed up as follows:—
1) Stupid fat Sally is the daughter of the Head of Education Committee.
2) The long range weather forecast.
3) Billy's father is twice your size.
4) The kitchen staff being entirely vegetarian.
Experienced teachers will add to the list over the years.

YOGA

Oriental forms of exercise are growing in popularity in societies where 'stress' is increasing. Personalised forms of exercise aimed at 'relaxing' the nervous system, of which Yoga is the best known, remind us of the need to help people 'switch off' as well as to 'switch on' (for great effort in sports events). A perusal of the personal columns of the New Statesman and other journals will reveal a number of persons and organisations teaching yoga.
RELAXATION

YOUTH

Whilst young people should be brought into the organisation and teaching of sports and physical education, early and fully, all responsibility should not be abandoned to them. There are young 90 years olds, and old 20 year olds, as we all know. *Youth* is truly an attitude of mind. Sport brings the different generations into contact with one another and perhaps helps adults to retain elements of youth which might otherwise be eliminated. Physical activity helps people to stay young longer.

YOUTH HOSTELLING

The only real way of getting to know the countryside is to walk, cycle, climb or travel by canoe. People who enjoy these activities are encouraged by the Youth Hostels Association (England and Wales) which exists to help all, especially young people of limited means, to a greater knowledge, love and care of the countryside. In particular hostels or other simple accommodation is provided for them in their travels, thus promoting their health, rest and education.

National Office: Youth Hostels Association (England and Wales), Trevelyan House, 8 St. Stephen's Hill, St Albans, Herts. Tel: St. Albans 55215

Also: Scottish Youth Hostel Association, 7 Glebe Crescent, Stirling, Stirlingshire. Tel: 0786 2821.

OUTDOOR ACTIVITIES

ZEST

This is what makes the person 'tick'—the child 'bubble'—the meal really 'taste'. The 18th century version of zest still has meaning today for a confectioner who uses zest when he cuts the peel of an orange or lemon from top to bottom into small strips, slicing it as thinly as it can be done. Certainly the analogy draws attention to the elusive quality of **zest** (the oils in the fruit skins which are the key factor in concocting drinks, food, lotions etc.) Who knows how much is in each fruit and who knows the untapped zest in a human? Only till keen relish and enjoyment appear, whether in speech or action can this gusto, this zest, be experienced. The teacher in physical education must have the ability to seek out with his own zest—the zest that lies within every child.

TALENT

ZOO

The institutions for displaying animals are now of more value than for merely the show of strange or beautiful species. As well as knowledge of behaviour, and metabolism and reproduction, much value for physical education can be obtained by studying the shape, form, patterns, sizes, colours and habitats of animals both for functional and expressive movement work. See 'Human Zoo' by Desmond Morris.

APPENDIX 1

LIST OF IMPORTANT ADDRESSES

CO-ORDINATING ORGANIZATIONS

SECRETARY AND ADDRESS

BRITISH OLYMPIC ASSOCIATION

K. S. Duncan, M.B.E.,
12 Buckingham Street,
London, W.C.2.

CENTRAL COUNCIL OF PHYSICAL RECREATION

H. Justin Evans, M.B.E., M.A.
(Acting General Secretary),
26 Park Crescent,
London, W.1.

HEALTH & STRENGTH LEAGUE

W. S. Pullum,
5 Church Street,
Camberwell,
London, S.E.5.

KEEP FIT ASSOCIATION OF ENGLAND AND WALES, THE

Mrs. Jose Griffiths,
46 Leith Mansions,
Grantully Road,
London,W.9.

KEEP FIT ASSOCIATION OF NORTHERN IRELAND

Miss A. Lyons,
7 Kingsberry Park,
Belfast 6.

MEDAU SOCIETY OF GREAT BRITAIN AND NORTHERN IRELAND

Miss M. Braithwaite,
85 Hampstead Way,
London, N.W.11.

SCOTTISH COUNCIL OF PHYSICAL RECREATION, THE

Mrs. M. Brown, M.B.E.,
4 Queensferry Street,
Edinburgh 2.

THE DALCROZE SOCIETY, INC.

Miss Lillian Linton,
66 Thames Eyot,
Twickenham,
Middx.

THE NATIONAL PLAYING FIELDS ASSOCIATION

Air Vice-Marshal R. A. Ramsay Rae,
C.B., O.B.E.,
57B Catherine Place,
London, S.W.1.

THE ROYAL ACADEMY OF DANCING

Miss M. Lehmann,
15 Holland Park Gardens
London, W.14.

THE SOCIETY FOR INTERNATIONAL FOLK DANCING

Miss M. Latham,
14 Beechwood Avenue,
Kew Gardens,
Surrey. Tel : PRO 7055

WOMEN'S LEAGUE OF HEALTH AND BEAUTY

Miss P. St. Lo,
Beaumont Cottage,
Ditton Close,
Thames Ditton,
Surrey.

FOCUS—(SPORTS ORGANISATION FOR STUDENTS OUTSIDE UNIVERSITIES)	B. Bellwood, Lecturer in P.E., Enfield College of Technology, Queenway, Enfield, Middx.
U.K. COMMITTEE FOR INTERNATIONAL CONFERENCES ABROAD	D. McNair, M.Ed., McDougall Centre, University, Manchester 13.
BRITISH UNIVERSITIES SPORTS FEDERATION	Woburn Square, London, W.C.1.
NATIONAL COUNCIL FOR SCHOOLS SPORTS	64 Winchester Road, Andover, Hants.
NATIONAL ASSOCIATION OF BOYS CLUBS	17 Bedford Square, London, W.C.1.
NATIONAL ASSOCIATION OF YOUTH CLUBS	30 Devonshire St., London, W.1.
DUKE OF EDINBURGH'S AWARD SCHEME	2 Old Queen Street, London, S.W.1.
OUTWARD BOUND TRUST	73 Gt. Peter St., London, S.W.1.
YOUTH HOSTELS ASSOCIATION	Trevelyan House, St. Albans, Herts.
BRITISH ASSOCIATION OF SPORTS AND MEDICINE	Dr. J. Williams, Farnham Park Rehabilitation Centre, Farnham Royal, Slough, Bucks.
ERGONOMICS RESEARCH SOCIETY	Prof. Floyd, Loughborough University, Loughborough, Leics.
UNIVERSITIES ATHLETICS UNION	R. Bottomley, 28 Woburn Square, London, W.C.1.
ENGLISH FOLK SONG AND DANCE SOCIETY	Cecil Sharp House, 2 Regent's Park Road, London, N.W.1.
BRITISH ASSOCIATION OF SPORTS COACHES	Chairman: T. McNab, 23 Crossway, Welwyn Garden City, Herts.
HEALTH FOUNDATION COUNCIL	Middlesex House, Ealing Road, Alperton, Wembley, Middx.
OFFICE OF HEALTH ECONOMICS	162 Regent Street, London, W.1.
ROYAL SOCIETY OF HEALTH	90 Buckingham Palace Road, London, S.W.1.

SCHOOLS' SPORTS
ORGANIZATIONS

BRITISH SCHOOLS JUDO
ASSOCIATION

Brian Saunders,
Pine Dene, Playford Mills,
Pilton
West, Barnstaple,
N. Devon.
(Girls' Section) : Miss Hazel Robbins,
36 Longacre Road,
Whitchurch,
Bristol 4.

ENGLISH SCHOOLS' FOOTBALL
ASSOCIATION

S. E. Tye,
126 Boston Manor Road,
Brentford, Middx.

NATIONAL SCHOOL SAILING
ASSOCIATION

Harry Cross,
County Hall,
Chichester,
Sussex.

SCHOOLS' AMATEUR BOXING
ASSOCIATION

A. J. P. Martin,
"Belview",
Belmont Road,
Maidenhead, Berkshire.

THE ASSOCIATION FOR ARCHERY
IN SCHOOLS

Miss M. Snelgrove,
121 Athelstan Road,
Bitterne,
Southampton.

THE BOYS' SCHOOLS LAWN
TENNIS ASSOCIATION

F. McL. Milbourn,
28 Maiden Erlegh Drive,
Earley, Reading,
Berks.

THE ENGLISH SCHOOLS'
ATHLETIC ASSOCIATION

J. Forrester, M.B.E.,
Dunelm, Horton Road,
Newbottle, Co. Durham.

THE ENGLISH SCHOOLS' BASKET
BALL ASSOCIATION

Philip G. Deadman,
Morrison Secondary Boys' School,
Rose Lane,
Liverpool 18.

THE ENGLISH SCHOOLS' CRICKET
ASSOCIATION

C. R. Hansford,
11 Coombe Rise,
Findon Valley,
Worthing, Sussex.
Tel. Findon 2089

THE SCHOOLS JUDO
ASSOCIATION

Brian Saunders,
Pine Dene,
Playford Mills,
Pilton West,
Barnstaple, N. Devon.

THE ENGLISH SCHOOLS
RUGBY ASSOCIATION

J. Spark,
12 Kennersdene,
Tynemouth,
Northumberland.
Tel. Shields 75107

THE ENGLISH SCHOOLS'
SWIMMING ASSOCIATION

S. Hartley,
106 Bocking Lane,
Sheffield 8, Yorks.

THE GIRLS' SCHOOLS LAWN TENNIS ASSOCIATION	Miss M. E. Parker, St. Michael's School, Limpsfield, Surrey.
THE SCOTTISH SCHOOLS ATHLETIC ASSOCIATION	A. C. Reld, 6 Merrylee Crescent, Giffnock, Glasgow.
ENGLISH SCHOOLS' VOLLEYBALL ASSOCIATION	R. Black, 16 Regent Avenue, Bowning Park, Liverpool 14.
THE NATIONAL COUNCIL FOR SCHOOLS' SPORTS	R. Charlton, O.B.E., J.P., 64 Winchester Road, Andover, Hants. (For addresses of other Schools Sports Associations newly formed.)

GOVERNING BODIES OF SPORT **SECRETARY AND ADDRESS**
ANGLING:

NATIONAL FEDERATION OF ANGLERS	T. G. Draper, 47 Lindon Drive, Alvaston, Derby.

ARCHERY:

GRAND NATIONAL ARCHERY SOCIETY THE,	John J. Bray, 20 Broomfield Road, Chelmsford, Essex.
SCOTTISH ARCHERY ASSOCIATION, THE	R. P. McKell, 41 Hunter Crescent, Troon.

85

ULSTER ARCHERY ASSOCIATION Captain Harold Higham,
342 Merville Garden Village,
Newtownabbey,
Co. Antrim,
Northern Ireland.

ASSOCIATION FOOTBALL:

FOOTBALL ASSOCIATION, THE Denis Follows, M.B.E., B.A.,
22 Lancaster Gate,
London, W.2.

FOOTBALL ASSOCIATION OF H. Powell, O.B.E.,
WALES LTD., THE 3 Fairy Road,
Wrexham.

IRISH FOOTBALL ASSOCIATION W. J. Drennan,
LTD. 20 Windsor Avenue,
Belfast,
Northern Ireland.

SCOTTISH FOOTBALL W. P. Allan, J.P.,
ASSOCIATION LTD. 6 Park Gardens,
Glasgow, C.3.

SCOTTISH AMATEUR FOOTBALL A. M. Macnab,
ASSOCIATION 75 Buchanan Street,
Glasgow, C.1.

ATHLETICS:

AMATEUR ATHLETIC B. E. Willis,
ASSOCIATION 26 Park Crescent,
London, W.1.

BRITISH UNIVERSITIES SPORTS Mrs. P. Besford, General Secretary
FEDERATION 28 Woburn Square,
London, W.C.1.

NORTHERN IRELAND AMATEUR J. L. Patton,
ATHLETIC ASSOCIATION 75 Glenburn Road,
Dunmurry.
Belfast, N.I.

NORTHERN IRELAND WOMEN'S Mrs. H. S. O'Neill,
AMATEUR ATHLETIC Rushden,
ASSOCIATION 5 Glenavon Park,
Jordanstown, Newtownabbey
Northern Ireland.

SCOTTISH AMATEUR ATHLETIC R. B. Forman,
ASSOCIATION, THE 14 Comiston Drive,
Edinburgh, 10.

SCOTTISH WOMEN'S AMATEUR Mrs. G. J. Brown,
ATHLETIC ASSOCIATION 28 Comiston Drive,
Edinburgh 10.

UNIVERSITIES ATHLETIC UNION R. W. Palmer,
28 Woburn Square,
London, W.1.

WOMEN'S AMATEUR ATHLETIC
ASSOCIATION

Miss M. Hartman, M.B.E.,
Hon. Secretary,
41 Hayward Court,
Levehurst Way, Clapham,
London, S.W.4.

WOMEN'S INTER-UNIVERSITY
ATHLETIC BOARD

Mrs. B. N. Nunns,
12 Crescent Road,
Sidcup, Kent.

BADMINTON:

BADMINTON ASSOCIATION OF
ENGLAND

H. A. E. Scheele,
4 Madeira Avenue,
Bromley, Kent.

NORTHERN BRANCH BADMINTON
UNION OF IRELAND

Major J. D. M. McCallum, C.B.E.,
D.S.O.,
41 Orminston Crescent,
Belfast.

SCOTTISH BADMINTON UNION,
THE

Craig Reedie,
1253 Argyle Street,
Glasgow, C.3.

BASKETBALL:

AMATEUR BASKETBALL
ASSOCIATION

K. K. Mitchell,
Dept. of Physical Education,
The University,
Leeds 2.

AMATEUR BASKETBALL
ASSOCIATION OF IRELAND
(ULSTER COUNCIL)

M. McCormack,
34 Norfolk Parade,
Belfast, 11.

AMATEUR BASKETBALL
ASSOCIATION OF SCOTLAND

R. McManson, C.A.,
c/o Foley,
18 Raeburn Place,
Edinburgh.

WELSH AMATEUR BASKETBALL
ASSOCIATION

I. Fryer,
4 Lyndhurst Street,
Mountain Ash,
Glamorgan.

BICYCLE POLO:

BICYCLE POLO ASSOCIATION
OF GREAT BRITAIN

H. L. Gray,
22 Hadley Road,
Mitcham, Surrey.

BICYCLE POLO ASSOCIATION
OF GREAT BRITAIN, THE

R. C. Allen
152 Bedford Hill,
London, S.W.12.

BILLIARDS:

BILLIARDS ASSOCIATION AND CONTROL COUNCIL, THE

Mrs. P. B. Holliday,
15 Exeter Street,
Strand, London, W.C.2.

BOWLING (TENPIN):

BRITISH TENPIN BOWLING ASSOCIATION

M. Glazer,
212 Lower Clapton Road,
London, E.5.

BOWLS:

ENGLISH BOWLING ASSOCIATION, THE

E. Sussum,
2 Roseford Road,
Cambridge.

BOXING:

AMATEUR BOXING ASSOCIATION, THE

W. T. Lovett,
Clutha House,
10 Storey's Gate,
London, S.W.1.

BRITISH BOXING BOARD OF CONTROL (1929)

E. J. Waltham,
Ramilies Buildings,
Hill's Place,
London, W.1.

IRISH AMATEUR BOXING ASSOCIATION (ULSTER COUNCIL)

S. Hays,
31 Smithfield,
Belfast.

SCHOOLS AMATEUR BOXING ASSOCIATION

A. J. P. Martin,
"Belview",
Belmont Road,
Maidenhead, Berks.

SCOTTISH AMATEUR BOXING ASSOCIATION

J. Henderson,
13 Blairhall Avenue,
Langside, Glasgow, S.1.

WELSH AMATEUR BOXING ASSOCIATION

V. Thomas Westhaven,
303 Davies Ave.,
West Park,
Nottage,
Porthcawl, Glam.

CAMPING:

CAMPING CLUB OF GREAT BRITAIN AND IRELAND, THE

G. A. Cubitt,
11 Lower Grosvenor Place
London, S.W.1.

YOUTH CAMPING ASSOCIATION

Mrs. G. Stallworthy,
26 Crown Lane,
Southgate, N.14.

CANOEING:

BRITISH CANOE UNION, THE

The General Secretary,
Room 316,
26/29 Park Crescent,
London, W.1.

CANOE-CAMPING CLUB, THE

The Secretary,
11 Lower Grosvenor Place,
London, S.W.1.

SCOTTISH CANOE ASSOCIATION

Charles Cousar,
26 Harbour Street,
Irvine, Ayrshire.

CRICKET:

CLUB CRICKET CONFERENCE, THE

Major S. W. Woods,
64a Hill Road,
London, S.W.19.

MARYLEBONE CRICKET CLUB, THE

S. C. Griffith,
Lord's Cricket Ground,
London, N.W.8.

M.C.C. YOUTH CRICKET ASSOCIATION

J. G. Dunbar, F.R.I.C.S.,
M.C.C., Lord's Cricket Ground,
London, N.W.8.

NATIONAL CLUB CRICKET ASSOCIATION

T. R. Kent,
28 Lawrence Road,
Hove, 3,
Sussex.

NORTHERN CRICKET UNION OF IRELAND

G. C. Ormsby,
58 Upper Queens Street,
Belfast 1.

SCOTTISH CRICKET UNION

G. Miller, C.A.,
41 Charlotte Square,
Edinburgh 3.

WOMEN'S CRICKET ASSOCIATION

Miss E. M. Riley,
Corner Farm,
Frittenden,
nr. Cranbrook, Kent.

CROQUET:

CROQUET ASSOCIATION, THE

Mrs. V. C. Gasson,
The Hurlingham Club,
London, S.W.6.

89

CROSS COUNTRY RUNNING:

ENGLISH CROSS-COUNTRY UNION

G. L. N. Dunn,
Woodlin, 5 Granta Terrace,
Stapleford, Cambridge.

CYCLING:

BRITISH CYCLING FEDERATION

Room 319,
26 Park Crescent,
London, W.1
National Coach: N. Sheil,
100 Valmont Road,
Bramcote, Notts.

CYCLISTS TOURING CLUB

Leslie C. Warner,
3 Craven Hill,
London, W.2.

CYCLISTS' TOURING CLUB (N.I. DISTRICT ASSOCIATION)

D. C. Loretto,
3 Gortin Drive, Belfast 5,
Northern Ireland.

ROAD TIME TRIALS COUNCIL, THE

E. G. Kings,
210 Devonshire Hill Lane,
London, N.17.

SCOTTISH CYCLISTS' UNION

James Leonard,
33 Benford Avenue,
Newarthill, Motherwell.

DANCING:

ENGLISH FOLK DANCE AND SONG SOCIETY, THE

K. F. Goode,
Cecil Sharp House,
2 Regent's Park Road,
London, N.W.1.

IMPERIAL SOCIETY OF TEACHERS OF DANCING, THE

P. J. Pearson, F.C.A.
70 Gloucester Place,
London, W.1.

MODERN MOVEMENT, INTERNATIONAL ASSOCIATION OF MARGARET MORRIS MOVEMENT

Mrs. I. M. Jeayes,
38 Trossachs Road,
London, S.E.22.

NATIONAL ASSOCIATION OF TEACHERS OF DANCING

D. Franklyn,
20 Mayplace Road West,
Bexleyheath, Kent.

NORTHERN IRELAND SOCIETY OF DANCE TEACHERS

Mrs. E. Delaney,
Upper Church Lane,
Belfast, Northern Ireland.

ROYAL ACADEMY OF DANCING, THE

Miss M. Lehmann,
General Secretary,
15 Holland Park Gardens,
London, W.11.

ROYAL SCOTTISH COUNTRY DANCE SOCIETY	Miss M. F Hadden, 12 Coates Crescent, Edinburgh 3.
SOCIETY FOR INTERNATIONAL FOLK DANCING	Mrs. M. Latham, 14 Beechwood Ave., Kew Gardens, Surrey.
WELSH FOLK DANCE SOCIETY	Mrs. F. Mon Jones, Bryntirion, Llanrhaedr, Y.M., nr. Oswestry, Salop.

EQUESTRIANISM:

| BRITISH HORSE SOCIETY | J. E. Blackmore, 16 Bedford Square, London, W.C.1. |
| BRITISH SHOW JUMPING ASSOCIATION, THE | Captain G. H. S. Webber 16 Bedford Square, London, W.C.1. |

FENCING:

AMATEUR FENCING ASSOCIATION, THE	Lieutenant Commander R. T. Forsdick, 83 Perham Road, West Kensington, London, W.14.
LADIES' AMATEUR FENCING UNION	Miss M. Somerville, 58a Ridgmount Gardens, London, W.C.1.
SCOTTISH AMATEUR FENCING UNION	J. L. Hope, 3 Ravelston Dykes Lane, Edinburgh 4.

FISHING:

FLYFISHERS' CLUB, THE	3 Whitehall Court, London, S.W.1.
LONDON ANGLERS' ASSOCIATION	R. S. D. Davison, F.C.C.S., 50 Elfindale Road, Herne Hill, London, S.E.24.
NATIONAL FEDERATION OF ANGLERS	T. G. Draper, 47 Lindon Drive, Alvaston, Derby

FIVES:

ETON FIVES ASSOCIATION

Hon. Sec. D. J. S. Guilford,
Baldwin's Shore,
Eton College,
Windsor, Berks.

RUGBY FIVES ASSOCIATION

D. E. Gardner,
51 Rafford Way,
Bromley, Kent.

GLIDING:

BRITISH GLIDING ASSOCIATION

Miss F. Leighton,
Artillery Mansions,
75 Victoria Street,
London, S.W.1.

SCOTTISH GLIDING UNION

A. R. Grieve,
Portmoak,
Scotlandwell, By Kinross,
Kinrossshire.

GOLF:

ENGLISH GOLF UNION

Lt.-Col. K. A. Nash,
35 Broad Street,
Wokingham, Berkshire.

GOLF FOUNDATION, THE

Lt.-Col. W. B. J. Armstrong,
2 St. James's Square,
London, S.W.1.

LADIES' GOLF UNION

Miss K. Hannay,
Sandilands,
Sandwich Bay, Kent.

ROYAL AND ANCIENT GOLF CLUB OF ST. ANDREWS

Brig. E. Brickman, D.S.O.,
St. Andrews,
Fife, Scotland.

SENIOR GOLFERS' SOCIETY

Captain F. B. Lloyd, O.B.E., R.N.
1 Morley Road,
Farnham, Surrey.

VETERAN LADIES' GOLF ASSOCIATION

Miss Eileen M. Wilson,
14 Devonshire House
Devonshire Avenue,
Sutton, Surrey.

GREYHOUND RACING:

GREYHOUND RACING ASSOCIATION LTD.

Reg Howell,
20 Berkeley Square,
London, W.1.

GYMNASTICS:

BRITISH AMATEUR GYMNASTICS
ASSOCIATION
F. Edmonds,
2 Ormesby Way,
Kenton, Harrow,
Middx

SCOTTISH AMATEUR GYMNASTIC
ASSOCIATION
I McB. Clegg,
115 Buccleugh Street,
Glasgow, C.3.

ULSTER AMATEUR GYMNASTIC
ASSOCIATION
F. Wilson,
10 The Mount,
Belfast.

HANDBALL

BRITISH HANDBALL ASSOCIATION
32 North John Street,
Liverpool, 2.

HOCKEY:

ALL ENGLAND WOMEN'S
HOCKEY ASSOCIATION
Mrs. M. Macdonald,
45 Doughty Street,
London, W.C.1

BRITISH HOCKEY BOARD
R. C. Tattersall,
White House Avenue Road,
Duffield, Derby.

HOCKEY ASSOCIATION, THE
R. J. W. Struthers,
26 Park Crescent,
London, W.1.

SCOTTISH HOCKEY ASSOCIATION
W. S. F Robertson, C.A.,
29 Whitehill Avenue,
Stepps, Glasgow.

SCOTTISH WOMEN'S HOCKEY
ASSOCIATION
Mrs. G. Richardson,
526 Anniesland Road,
Glasgow, W.3.

ULSTER BRANCH, IRISH
HOCKEY UNION
O. W. Peacock,
28 Cairnburn Road,
Belfast 4.

ULSTER WOMEN'S HOCKEY
UNION
Mrs. H. W. Templeton, M.B.E.,
36 Ardenlee Avenue,
Belfast 6.

WELSH HOCKEY ASSOCIATION
K. H. Ingledew,
9 Cathedral Road.
Cardiff.

WELSH WOMEN'S HOCKEY
ASSOCIATION
Miss Norma Roblin,
107 Montermer Road,
Cardiff.

ICE HOCKEY:

BRITISH ICE HOCKEY
ASSOCIATION LIMITED,
(BY GUARANTEE)
J. F. Ahearne,
Empire House,
175 Piccadilly,
London, W.1.

JUDO:

BRITISH JUDO ASSOCIATION,
THE

Miss P. J. Hogg,
26/29 Park Crescent,
London, W.1.

SCOTTISH JUDO UNION

S. Kingalis,
101 Albion Street,
Glasgow, 5.

LACROSSE:

ALL ENGLAND WOMEN'S
LACROSSE ASSOCIATION

Miss P. M. Wookey,
26 Park Crescent,
London, W.1.

ALL WALES LADIES' LACROSSE
ASSOCIATION

Miss J. Donovan,
51 St. Nicholas Road,
Barry.

ENGLISH LACROSSE UNION

C. D. Coppock,
3 Chessington Avenue,
Bexleyheath, Kent.

SCOTTISH LADIES' LACROSSE
ASSOCIATION

Mrs. A. Dunhill,
29 Lygon Road,
Edinburgh 9.

LAWN TENNIS:

LAWN TENNIS ASSOCIATION, THE

S. B. Reay, O.B.E.,
The Lawn Tennis Association,
Barons Court,
London, W.14.

SCOTTISH LAWN TENNIS
ASSOCIATION

D. D. Carmichael,
1 Royal Terrace,
Edinburgh 7.

IRISH LAWN TENNIS
ASSOCIATION, THE
(ULSTER COUNCIL)

Dr. J. O. Darbyshire, M.A.,
4 Glen Road,
Jordanstown,
Newtown Abbey,
Co. Antrim.

LAWN TENNIS FOUNDATION, THE

The Manager, Jack Moore,
Queen's Club, Baron's Court,
London, W.14.

MODERN PENTATHLON:

MODERN PENTATHLON
ASSOCIATION OF GREAT BRITAIN

J. D. Majendie,
Rose Cottage,
Platt, Sevenoaks,
Kent.

MOTOR CYCLING:

AUTO-CYCLE UNION

K. E. Shierson,
31 Belgrave Square,
London, S.W.1.

MOTORING:

AUTOMOBILE ASSOCIATION

Director-General,
Fanum House,
Leicester Square,
London, W.C.2.

ROYAL AUTOMOBILE CLUB

Cdr. D. P. Little, R.N.,
Pall Mall,
London, S.W 1.

MOUNTAINEERING:

ALPINE CLUB

74 South Audley Street.
London, W.1.

*BRITISH MOUNTAINEERING
COUNCIL, THE*

H. D. Greenwood,
c/o Alpine Club,
74 South Audley Street,
London, W.1.

*IRISH MOUNTAINEERING CLUB
(BELFAST SECTION)*

Miss Michele Ramsey,
37 Cyprus Gardens,
Belfast.

*MOUNTAINEERING ASSOCIATION,
THE*

J. E. B. Wright,
102a Westbourne Grove,
London, W.2.

NETBALL:

*ALL ENGLAND NETBALL
ASSOCIATION*

Miss A. Cairncross,
Room 314,
26/29 Park Crescent,
London, W.1.

*NORTHERN IRELAND NETBALL
ASSOCIATION*

Miss Maureen Gray,
26 Agra Street,
Belfast 7.

*SCOTTISH NETBALL ASSOCIATION,
THE*

Miss M. Getty,
30 Melville Street,
Pollokshields, Glasgow.

WELSH NETBALL ASSOCIATION

Miss M. Williams,
91 Park Place,
Gilfach, Bargoed,
Glamorgan.

OLYMPIC GAMES:

BRITISH OLYMPIC ASSOCIATION
K. S. Duncan, M.B.E.,
12 Buckingham Street,
London, W.C.2.

ORIENTEERING:

ENGLISH ORIENTEERING ASSOCIATION
Gerry Charnley,
9 St. Stephens Road,
Hightown,
Liverpool.

GLOUCESTER COMMITTEE FOR ORIENTEERING
J. Thomas,
18 Suffolk Road,
Cheltenham, Glos.

NORTH MIDLANDS ORIENTEERING ASSOCIATION
W. T. Hamilton,
People's College of Further Education,
Castle Road, Nottingham.

NORTH WESTERN ORIENTEERING
G. Charnley,
9 St. Stephen's Road,
Hightown,
Liverpool, Lancs.

SCOTTISH ORIENTEERING ASSOCIATION
Colin Cruikshank,
The Pollock Institute,
Pleasance,
Edinburgh 8.

SOUTH RIBBLE ORIENTEERING CLUB
K. Turner,
3 Werneth Close,
Flag Lane, Penwortham,
Preston, Lancs.

SOUTHERN NAVIGATORS, CLUB, THE
C. Brasher,
The Navigator's House,
River Lane. Petersham,
Surrey.

WEST MIDLANDS ORIENTEERING ASSOCIATION
A. Batstone,
Bourneville College of Further Education,
Bourneville, Birmingham.

PONY POLO:

HURLINGHAM POLO ASSOCIATION, THE
Brig. J. R. C. Gannon, C.B.E., M.V.O.,
and Lt.-Col. A F. Logan, M.C.
137 Victoria Street,
London. S.W.1.

PONY TREKKING:

PONY TREKKING ASSOCIATION
Caeglas, Llanwrtyd Wells,
Breconshire.

PONIES OF BRITAIN
Mrs. Glenda Spooner,
Brookside Farm,
Ascot, Berks.

RACE WALKING:

RACE WALKING ASSOCIATION
L. W. Woodcock,
191 Amesbury Avenue,
Streatham Hill,
London, S.W.2.

RAMBLING:

RAMBLERS' ASSOCIATION
T. Stephenson,
124 Finchley Road,
London, N.W.3.

RIDING:

BRITISH HORSE SOCIETY, THE
J. E. Blackmore,
16 Bedford Square
London, W.C.1.

ROUNDERS:

*NATIONAL ROUNDERS
ASSOCIATION*
Miss B. A. Furlong,
81 King Harold Road,
Colchester, Essex.

ROWING:

*AMATEUR ROWING
ASSOCIATION*
J. H. Page, O.B.E., T.D.,
Room 321,
26/29 Park Crescent,
London, W.1.
(*LAN.* 0854)

*SCOTTISH AMATEUR ROWING
ASSOCIATION*
G. A. Hunter,
18 Campbellpark Crescent,
Colinton,
Edinburgh 13.

*WOMENS' AMATEUR ROWING
COUNCIL*
Miss J. Filkins,
20 Wensleydale Road,
Hampton, Middlesex.

RUGBY LEAGUE FOOTBALL:

RUGBY FOOTBALL LEAGUE
W. Fallowfield, O.B.E., M.A.,
180 Chapeltown Road,
Leeds 7

RUGBY UNION FOOTBALL:

RUGBY FOOTBALL UNION

The Secretary,
Whitton Road,
Twickenham, Middx.

IRISH RUGBY FOOTBALL UNION,
ULSTER BRANCH

T. J. Rothwell, B.E.M.,
Ravenhill Park,
Belfast 6.

WELSH RUGBY UNION

W. H. Clement,
Royal London House,
28-31 St. Mary Street,
Cardiff.

SAILING:

THE SAIL TRAINING
ASSOCIATION

Col. R. G. F. Scholfield,
Ferndown,
Hill Brow,
Liss. Hants.

SHOOTING:

CLAY PIGEON SHOOTING
ASSOCIATION

A. P. Page,
Eley Estate,
Angel Road,
Edmonton, London, N.18.

NATIONAL RIFLE ASSOCIATION

Captain E. K. LeMesurier, C.B.E.,
M.V O., R.N. (Retd.),
Bisley Camp,
Brookwood,
Woking, Surrey.

NATIONAL SMALL-BORE RIFLE
ASSOCIATION, THE

A. J. Palmer,
Codrington House,
113 Southwark Street,
London, S.E.1.

THE JOINT SHOOTING
COMMITTEE FOR GREAT
BRITAIN

A. J. Palmer,
Codrington House,
133 Southwark St.,
London, S.E.1.

SKATING:

NATIONAL ROLLER HOCKEY
ASSOCIATION

W. W. Kimber,
35 Olive Road,
London, N.W.2.

NATIONAL SKATING ASSOCIATION
OF GREAT BRITAIN

E. G. Coggins, O.B.E.,
Charterhouse,
London, E.C.1

SCOTTISH AMATEUR ICE SPEED SKATING ASSOCIATION	D. McCallum, 26 High Street, Paisley, Renfrewshire.

SKI-ING:

SCOTTISH SKI CLUB, THE	R. R. E. Pender, B.I., 257 West Campbell Street, Glasgow, C.2.
NATIONAL SKI FEDERATION OF GREAT BRITAIN, THE	M. N. H. Milne, O.B.E., E.D., M.A., 118 Eaton Square, London, S.W.1.

SQUASH RACKETS:

SCOTTISH SQUASH RACKETS ASSOCIATION	O. L. Balfour, 79 Craiglockhart Road, South, Edinburgh 11.
SQUASH RACKETS ASSOCIATION, THE	J. H. Horry, 26 20 Park Crescent, London, W.1.
WOMENS' SQUASH RACKETS ASSOCIATION	Mrs. A. M. Fisk, 22 Childebert Road, London, S.W.17.

SUB-AQUA:

BRITISH SUB-AQUA CLUB, THE	Major H. Wallace, 25 Orchard Road, Kingston upon Thames, Surrey.

SWIMMING:

AMATEUR SWIMMING ASSOCIATION	Alderman H. E. Fern, C.B.E., J.P., 64 Cannon Street, London, E.C.4.
BRITISH SWIMMING COACHES ASSOCIATION	G. E. Bole, 26 Whitby Avenue, Fartown, Huddersfield.
ROYAL LIFE SAVING SOCIETY	Brigadier P. de C. Jones, O.B.E., Desborough House, 14 Devonshire Srteet, Portland Place, London, W.1.

SWIMMING TEACHERS'
ASSOCIATION OF GREAT BRITAIN
AND THE COMMONWEALTH
(INCORPORATED)

R. Clements, D.S.T.A., A.I.A.C.,
34 Tiverton Close,
High Acres,
Kingswinford, Staffs.

ULSTER BRANCH OF THE IRISH
AMATEUR SWIMMING
ASSOCIATION

J. Stevenson,
5 Hillside Drive,
Belfast 9,
Northern Ireland.

WELSH AMATEUR SWIMMING
ASSOCIATION

W. Hooper,
45 Devon Place,
Newport, Mon.

TABLE TENNIS:

ENGLISH TABLE TENNIS
ASSOCIATION

D. Peter Lowen,
652 Grand Buildings,
Trafalgar Square,
London, W.C.2.

IRISH TABLE TENNIS
ASSOCIATION (ULSTER BRANCH)

W. J. Kidd,
65 Breda Road,
Belfast 8.

SCOTTISH TABLE TENNIS
ASSOCIATION

R. D. Dykes,
99 Henderson Row,
Edinburgh 3.

TABLE TENNIS ASSOCIATION
OF WALES

Mrs. H. Roy Evans,
1 Llwyn-y-Grant Road,
Cyncoed, Cardiff.

TENNIS AND RACKETS:

TENNIS AND RACKETS
ASSOCIATION

Jt. Hon. Secs.
Col. N. S. Renny, O.B.E.,
Ashley Court South,
Ashtead, Surrey.
J. R. Greenwood, J.P.,
Stonehall, Bothcombe,
Sussex

TRAMPOLINING:

BRITISH TRAMPOLINE
FEDERATION

Rob Walker,
c/o P.E. Department,
The Polytechnic,
309 Regent Street,
London, W.1.

VOLLEYBALL:

AMATEUR VOLLEYBALL
ASSOCIATION OF GREAT
BRITAIN

R. Pankhurst,
General Secretary,
Southgate Technical College,
High Street, London, N.14.

WATER SKIING:

THE BRITISH WATER SKI
FEDERATION

A. Richardson, Egham, Surrey.

WEIGHT-LIFTING:

BRITISH AMATEUR WEIGHT-
LIFTERS' ASSOCIATION

W. Holland,
223 Iffley Road,
Oxford.

SCOTTISH AMATEUR WEIGHT-
LIFTERS' ASSOCIATION

J. B. Sillers,
370 Peat Road,
Nitshill, Glasgow, S.W.3.

WRESTLING:

BRITISH AMATEUR WRESTLING
ASSOCIATION, THE

A. Wishart,
60 Calabria Road,
London, N.5.

SCOTTISH AMATEUR WRESTLING
ASSOCIATION

T. B. McMillan,
5 Hinchelwood Drive,
Glasgow, S.W.1.

YACHTING:

ROYAL YACHTING ASSOCIATION

F. P. Usborne, M.B E.,
171 Victoria Street,
London, S.W.1.

AFFILIATED SOCIETIES GREAT BRITAIN

SECRETARY AND ADDRESS

ASSOCIATION OF P.E. LECTURERS IN COLLEGES OF FURTHER EDUCATION

C. H. Minta, Esq.,
Technical College and Institute of
Technology,
Manchester Road,
Bolton, Lancs.

NORTHERN IRELAND PHYSICAL EDUCATION ASSOCIATION

Miss S. Boyd,
1 Priory Park,
Belfast 10,
N. Ireland.

SCOTTISH ASSOCIATION FOR PHYSICAL EDUCATION (MEN).

Robert McLaren,
185 MacGregor Road,
Cumbernauld, Dunbartonshire,
Scotland.

SCOTTISH LEAGUE FOR PHYSICAL EDUCATION (WOMEN).

Miss M. Reid,
8 Westfield Drive,
Greenrock, Renfrewshire.

THE UNIVERSITIES PHYSICAL EDUCATION ASSOCIATION

R. St. G. T. Harper, Esq., M.A.,
Director of Department of P.E.,
The University,
Manchester 13.

WELSH ASSOCIATION OF PHYSICAL EDUCATION

Mrs. C. A. Mynott,
51 Lon Isa,
Rhiwbina, Cardiff.

TERRITORIAL ASSOCIATIONS

BERKSHIRE ASSOCIATION FOR PHYSICAL EDUCATION

R. S. C. Sharp, Esq.,
31 Matlock Road,
Caversham,
Reading, Berks.

BIRMINGHAM AND DISTRICT PHYSICAL EDUCATION ASSOCIATION

Miss E. M. Richfield,
West Midlands Training College,
Gorway, Walsall,
Staffs.

BOURNEMOUTH AND DISTRICT PHYSICAL EDUCATION ASSOCIATION

Miss M. Vizard,
Uplands School,
Sandecotes Road,
Parkstone,
Poole, Dorset.

BRISTOL AND DISTRICT PHYSICAL EDUCATION ASSOCIATION

Mrs. D. L. Lane,
18 Blenheim Road,
Redland, Bristol 6.

DEVON PHYSICAL EDUCATION ASSOCIATION

W. Ewing, Esq.,
The Primary School,
Aveton Gifford,
Kingsbridge, S. Devon.

HERTFORDSHIRE PHYSICAL EDUCATION ASSOCIATION

S. H. Kemp, Esq.,
Stevenage College of F.E
Monkswood Way,
Stevenage, Herts.

*HULL AND EAST RIDING
PHYSICAL EDUCATION
ASSOCIATION*

T. P. Jones, Esq.,
378 Bricknell Avenue,
Hull.

*LEEDS AND DISTRICT PHYSICAL
EDUCATION ASSOCIATION*

Mrs. C. D. Firth,
160 Reevy Road,
Bradford 6.

*LIVERPOOL AND DISTRICT
PHYSICAL EDUCATION
ASSOCIATION*

Miss G. Priestley,
Education Offices,
14 Sir Thomas Street,
Liverpool 1.

*MANCHESTER AND DISTRICT
PHYSICAL EDUCATION
ASSOCIATION*

Miss K. Smith,
22 Broomhall Road,
Higher Blackley,
Manchester 9.

*NORTH EASTERN PHYSICAL
EDUCATION ASSOCIATION*

Miss L. Groves,
St. Hild's College,
Durham.

*NORTH WESTERN COUNTIES
PHYSICAL EDUCATION
ASSOCIATION*

D. McNair, Esq., M.Ed.,
Dept. of P.E.,
University of Manchester
Manchester 13.

*NOTTINGHAM AND
NOTTINGHAMSHIRE PHYSICAL
EDUCATION ASSOCIATION*

Miss M. Rawson,
21 Allendale Avenue,
Aspley, Nottingham.

*QUEEN ALEXANDRA'S HOUSE
PHYSICAL TRAINING COLLEGE
OLD STUDENTS' ASSOCIATION*

Miss B. E. Dreschfield,
Ford's Fields,
Smuggler's Lane,
Crowborough, Sussex.

*SURREY PHYSICAL
EDUCATION ASSOCIATION*

Mrs. A. Hudson,
Campions, Chalk Lane,
East Horsley, Surrey.

APPENDIX II

PERIODICALS ON SPORT AND
PHYSICAL RECREATION

1.   British Journal of Physical Education,
      Physical Education Association,
      Ling House,
      10, Nottingham Place,
      London, W.1.

2.   Sport and Recreation,
      C.C.P.R.,
      26 Park Crescent,
      London, W.1.

3.   World Sports,
      British Olympic Association,
      12 Buckingham Street,
      London, W.C.1.

4.   Scottish Journal of Physical Education.

5.   Bulletin of the BAOLPE.

From United States of America.
1.   Journal of Health, Physical Education and Recreation (JOPHER)
      1201 16th St., N.W.,
      Washington D.C. 20036

2.   Sports Illustrated,
      Rockefeller Centre,
      New York,
      N.Y. 10020

International:
1.   "Gymnasion", "Revue analytique",

2.   and "International Revue of Sports Sociology".
      from :   Bureau of Documentation,   (This Bureau plans a YEAR-
                87, rue Louvrex,   BOOK on Sport and Physical
                Liège, Belgium.   Education)

3.   Journal of Sports Medicine and Physical Fitness,
      Foro Italico,
      Rome, Italy.

4.   Bulletin of the International Olympic Committee,
      Chateau Vidy,
      Lausanne, Switzerland.

5.   Journal of the International Council of Military Sport (CISM)
      119 ave Franklin Roosevelt,
      Brussels 5, Belgium.

6.   Bulletins and Newsletters of all international sports federations and
      physical education organisations separately.

7.   Journals of many National Olympic Committees (DDR, Bulgaria
      for example) published in English.

APPENDIX III

ADDRESSES OF INTERNATIONAL ORGANISATIONS

1. IOC, Mon Repos, Lausanne, Switzerland.

2. PGA/NOC, Foro Italico, Rome, Italy (National Olympic Committees)

3. GAIF (International Sports Federations), 12 Avenue Valmont, 1010 Lausanne, Switzerland.

4. CISM, 119 Avenue Franklin Roosevelt, Brussels 5 (Military Sport).

5. AIPS (Sports Writers), 124 rue Reamur, Paris, France.

6. IAKS (Sports Facilities) Institute für Sportstättenbau, Sporthochschule, Carl Diem, Weg. Cologne-Mungersdorf, Germany F.R.

7. FISU (Student Sport) boulevard de Tervuren 101, Louvain, Belgium.

8. IAPESGW (Women's Sport), c/o Professor L. Diem, Sportshochschule, Cologne.

9. IRA (International Recreation Association), 345, East 46 St., New York, N.Y. 10017.

10. FIMS (Sports Medicine), Fore Italico, Rome, Italy.

11. ICHPER (Teachers) 1201 16th St., N.W. Washington, D.C., U.S.A.

12. AIESEPS (High Schools of Physical Education), 87 rue Louvrex, Liège, Belgium.

13. FIEP (International Physical Education Association), ave 5 do Outubro, 50 r/c-D to Lisbon, Portugal (Individuals).

14. ICSPE c/o Division of Youth Activities, Unesco House, Place de Fontenoy, Paris 7e, France.

    President: Rt. Hon. P. J. Noel-Baker, M.P.,
                        16 South Eaton Place, London, S.W.1.

    General Secretary: Dr. J. Falize,
                        Institut d'Education Physique,
                        87 rue Louvrex, Liège, Belgium.

    Deputy Secretary: D. W. J. Anthony, M.Ed.,
                        Avery Hill College of Education,
                        London, S.E.9.

EXTRACTS FROM THE HEALTH EDUCATION COUNCIL REPORT

"The objects for which the Council is established are to promote and encourage in England, Wales and Northern Ireland education and research in the science and art of healthy living and the principles of hygiene and the teaching thereof, and to assist Government Departments, local authorities and other statutory and voluntary bodies in so far as their work comprises health education and propaganda directed to the promotion or safeguarding of public health or to the prevention and cure of disease, and to provide analogous services for bodies and for individuals overseas. . . . ."

SMOKING AND HEALTH

A major anti-smoking poster campaign was launched in October 1969. This took the form of a national poster hoarding display which ran for three months. The message and its presentation were based on research into attitudes and beliefs on smoking and health by smokers, non-smokers, and ex-smokers. The poster design was selected from several pre-tested for their effectiveness in putting their message across. The evaluation of the campaign in terms of the effectiveness of the poster in changing attitudes and behaviour to smoking is still being carried out. Apart from the national poster sitings, over 90,000 copies of this poster in double crown and crown folio sizes were made available to local authorities in support of their own local anti-smoking health education activities.

FACTS ABOUT VD

A major campaign aimed at helping young people to develop their knowledge of the mode of transmission and the effects of gonorrhoea is under way. The communication problems presented by such a campaign were first explored by examining the comprehension and acceptability of the facts of gonorrhoea by depth interviews. These were conducted among a random sample of teen-agers and their parents. This study revealed a marked degree of misunderstanding about the disease amongst youngsters which required correction as an integral part of the communication process. The study also showed that youngsters were prepared to accept straight factual information of a bold type in preference to conventional evasive euphemisms.

DENTAL HEALTH

The main activity within the field of dental health has been an information campaign on fluoridation. The recently published 11-year report of the Committee on Research into Fluoridation was supplemented by the Council's own publication "Our Teeth". Approximately 13,000 copies of this publication and some 400 posters on the same theme have already been distributed. The press, radio, and television are being provided with factual information about flourida-tion, and the Council has set up an enquiry service.

THE INFECTIOUS DISEASES

Anticipating a measles epidemic during the winter of 1968/9 a press advertising campaign was mounted, supported by local editorial and feature material for newspapers. This was aimed at the mothers of unprotected children in an attempt to curtail the expected epidemic. Unfortunately one of the vaccines had to be withdrawn in the course of the campaign, but there is some indirect evidence to show that even so the increased number of children who were vaccinated resulted in a lower incidence of cases of measles.

The sporadic appearance of influenza during the same winter required public education. A co-ordinated campaign involving posters, leaflets, commissioned press articles, features, and editorial material was made available nationally and locally. This campaign was aimed at giving simple advice and reassurance about self-diagnosis and treatment.

A new poster and supporting leaflet urging infant immunisation against the common infectious diseases were made available during the year.

FOOD HYGIENE

A new television filmlet aimed at the mothers of young children and relating to personal hygiene is now being screened by both major networks. Two new posters were commissioned and are in circulation. Both have received considerable acclaim from the professional advertising world for their verbal boldness and communication effectiveness.

HOME ACCIDENTS

Attention has been focused upon accidental poisoning in the home. A grant from the Association of British Pharmaceutical Industries has allowed a TV filmlet on accidental medicinal poisoning in the home to be produced. A supportive poster on the related topic of accidental poisoning by domestic fluids is available.

CANCER EDUCATION

It seems that the Council's role at present is to provide general support on a national basis and to encourage newly emerging bodies—particularly locally.

A new leaflet on self-examination of the breasts is now available for distribution.

NUTRITION

It had been put to the Council that the mass educational approach to nutrition, virtually unchanged for a quarter of a century, should be reviewed in the light of modern knowledge and contemporary social patterns.

PRE-RETIREMENT EDUCATION

After a good deal of preliminary planning with the Pre-Retirement Association an experimental course has been held for doctors involved in pre-retirement education. Its aim was to develop a more effective approach by such doctors in their teaching methods and in the content of advice given to people in preparation for retirement. The Council, the Association and the Department of Education of the University of Leicester are now jointly concerned in preparing new courses based upon this experience.

SEX EDUCATION

A national conference to discuss how to achieve a coherent approach to sex education was held at the Royal College of Obstetricians and Gynaecologists in May 1970. This was planned with the help of the Council's Sex Education Advisory Panel. It contained contributions from the fields of education, clinical psychology, sociology, social anthropology, and the medical sciences. The aim was to bring before the many diverse, and often pre-committed, bodies in this field, the most important recent factual advances which relate to their interests and which may affect their thinking and actions in the coming years; and to discuss the possibility of setting up some form of joint standing body to co-ordinate national activities.

APPENDIX V

CARE OF EQUIPMENT (A PERSONAL VIEW)

I am only in a position to write authoritatively about equipment manufactured by my own company but I feel sure that no-one in the sports equipment industry would take exception to any advice I can offer.

An incident which occurred several years ago will serve to illustrate what is perhaps the first point about equipment care on a large scale. I was visiting a school at the time and discussing equipment with one of the physical education teachers. To illustrate the points that were being made he unlocked, and opened, a vast double cupboard which was neatly laid out with shelves of equipment, all nice and clean, and very well kept indeed. This of course was quite excellent in intention but to my horror I noticed that the cupboard was built across the main hot water pipe of a central heating system. The store cupboard was, as it happened, a veritable drying out cupboard. Here then is rule 1—*sports equipment should be kept in a cool dry place.*

Rule 2—*sports equipment should never ever be put away wet.* Apart from dampness caused by rain this includes the sweat that can be left by the hand on say the handle of a racket or bat. Handles of all sorts should be wiped down; tennis balls used on a damp day laid out to dry before storing, similarly with cricket pads; sports shoes, kept in a school locker, dried before locking up;—and so on.

Cleanliness is an important psychological factor but has a practical side as well. People who keep their sports equipment clean come to have a pride in their bat, racket or what have you— which seems in turn to help the inner man play or perform just that little bit better. What tennis player doesn't feel he is playing better with clean tennis balls? On the practical side properly cleaned equipment can often give advance warning of damage, or rather the cleaner is more likely to spot the warning signs. Rule 3—*sports equipment should be cleaned regularly.*

Rule 3 really leads directly into rule 4—*damage to equipment should receive immediate attention not allowed to go another game, another week, or until the end of term.* Of course as a marketing man I am only too happy to sell new equipment as regularly as possible but my colleagues and I find it very sad to see irretreivably damaged equipment which could obviously have been saved if caught early enough.

To summarize, the four basic rules that I would lay down for equipment care on a large scale are:

1) Store in a cool dry place.
2) Never put away wet.
3) Clean and examine regularly.
4) Damage, however slight, should receive immediate attention.

Having laid down the rules there are two rather more general points I would like to make. I think it is true to say that, without exception, the top performers in any sport you care to mention are always immaculately turned out for the game. Now I know that sports clothes cost money which pupils cannot afford but even so children can be encouraged to take a pride in their self presentation for games. It all comes back to the inner man I was talking about under rule 3; pride in oneself and one's equipment is a great psychological starter. Next time you have a match against another school why not suggest to the team that they will start with an advantage if they turn out really clean and smart, right down to the boots,—and, on the day, tell them that they look good; make them feel 'grand' about it before the game starts. Needless to say you will have to live up to the standard yourself!

The other point I would like to make also impinges upon the availability of finance but is something I would like to draw to your attention. I refer to the question of relating equipment to the size and strength of the pupil. I personally have seen cricket being played at a school where the bats were really of a size and weight appropriate to children a good five years older than the particular group in question. Now I accept that it is better to play cricket in these circumstances than not at all; I also accept that there would be no physical harm to the children (an overweight tennis racket on the other hand could perhaps cause physical harm.); and I also accept that the children were thoroughly enjoying themselves. On the other hand I would suggest that with an oversize cricket bat the pupil cannot gain, or be taught, the glorious feel of the correct stroke. It will be exercise, it will be fun, but it will not be catching the fire and the zest of the game for many years ahead.

Still on size but in a very different way I would like to be categoric on one final point. Undersize footwear used regularly in an energetic games situation can be very, very bad for the feet. On the other hand oversize footwear can be dangerous. If I only leave one point firmly in your minds let it be this one—in an energetic games or exercise situation a correct size of footwear is essential for the physical good of the pupil.

TONY CARTER
MARKETING DIRECTOR
DUNLOP SPORTS COMPANY LIMITED

SCOTTISH COUNCIL OF PHYSICAL RECREATION

None of the members of the editorial group were in a position to be able to provide notes on the 'Scottish Council of Physical Recreation'. As we felt that this would be an unfortunate omission we asked David Webster, a senior technical officer of the Council, to provide a brief note for the book.

EDITORS

The Scottish Council of Physical Recreation is an incorporated national voluntary organisation operating in Scotland whose main aims are to provide opportunities for all ages, to increase their knowledge of games, sports and a variety of leisure time activities, to encourage participation in these activities and to stimulate the provision of proper facilities.

The S.C.P.R. co-operates with its membership of over 150 national associations and 50 Individual Members—with education and other local authorities, industrial firms, colleges and universities, tourist and other agencies to provide training courses for coaches and leaders and sports coaching holidays for the general public.

The provision of good recreational facilities for the community has been one of the Council's priorities in recent years. Technical information and advice is freely given to those providing such amenities and the S.C.P.R. Technical Officers are regularly consulted by architects, local authority officials and elected members, and representatives of industrial concerns engaged in the provision of sporting and recreational facilities.

Scotland is rich in natural facilities and this is one of the main reasons why the Council has placed an emphasis on sports that can be practiced in lochs, mountains, rivers, the sea and in forest country. In this respect of its work, the S.C.P.R. co-operates with the Scottish Tourist Board to provide information and advice on ski-ing, angling, sailing, water ski-ing, pony trekking, canoeing, golf, gliding, mountaineering, sea angling, yacht cruising, etc. In this connection, safety in sport has been stressed and the Council emphasises water safety and mountain safety on a national scale.

The Council administers two National Recreation Centres— "Glenmore Lodge", the Scottish Centre for outdoor training which stands 1000' above sea level amid the pine-clad foothills of the Cairngorm mountains, and "Inverclyde", the Games, Sports and Outdoor Activities Centre on the West coast overlooking the Firth of Clyde, the Cumbraes, Arran and Bute. A Water Sports Centre for Scotland is planned for the foreseeable future.

The Council's offices in Edinburgh and Glasgow are vital centres of information. Those wishing to know more about a particular activity or sport anywhere in Scotland should contact the H.Q. office, 4 Queensferry Street, Edinburgh.

APPENDIX VII

TABLE 1

CONVERSION TABLES

M.	Ft.	Ins.	M.	Ft.	Ins.	M.	Ft.	Ins.	M.	Ft.	Ins.
1.50	4	11.06	21.00	68	10.79	54.50	178	9.71	74.00	242	9.45
2.00	6	6.75	21.50	70	6.48	55.00	180	5.40	74.50	244	5.13
2.50	8	2.43	36.00	118	1.35	55.50	182	1.08	75.00	246	0.82
3.00	9	10.11	36.50	119	9.04	56.00	183	8.77	75.50	247	8.51
3.50	11	5.80	37.00	121	4.72	56.50	185	4.45	76.00	249	4.19
4.00	13	1.47	37.50	123	0.40	57.00	187	0.14	76.50	250	11.86
4.50	14	9.17	38.00	124	8.09	57.50	188	7.82	77.00	252	7.56
5.00	16	4.85	38.50	126	3.77	58.00	190	3.51	77.50	254	3.24
5.50	18	0.54	39.00	127	11.47	58.50	191	11.19	78.00	255	10.93
6.00	19	8.23	39.50	129	7.16	59.00	193	6.88	78.50	257	6.61
6.50	21	3.91	40.00	131	2.87	59.50	195	0.56	79.00	259	2.30
7.00	22	11.59	40.50	132	10.52	60.00	196	10.26	79.50	260	9.98
7.50	24	7.28	41.00	134	6.29	60.50	198	5.94	80.00	262	5.68
8.00	26	2.96	41.50	136	1.89	61.00	200	1.63	80.50	264	1.37
8.50	27	10.65	42.00	137	9.58	61.50	201	9.31	81.00	265	9.05
9.00	29	6.34	42.50	139	5.26	62.00	203	5.00	81.50	267	4.73
9.50	31	2.02	43.00	141	0.95	62.50	205	0.69	82.00	269	0.42
10.00	32	9.71	43.50	142	8.63	63.00	206	8.37	82.50	270	8.10
10.50	34	5.39	44.00	144	4.32	63.50	208	4.05	83.00	272	3.79
11.00	36	1.08	44.50	146	0.00	64.00	209	11.74	83.50	273	11.47
11.50	37	8.77	45.00	147	7.69	64.50	211	7.42	84.00	275	7.16
12.00	39	4.45	45.50	149	3.37	65.00	213	3.11	84.50	277	2.84
12.50	41	0.13	46.00	150	11.06	65.50	214	10.79	85.00	278	10.53
13.00	42	7.82	46.50	152	6.74	66.00	216	6.48	85.50	280	6.21
13.50	44	3.50	47.00	154	2.43	66.50	218	2.16	86.00	282	1.90
14.00	45	11.19	47.50	155	10.11	67.00	219	9.85	86.50	283	9.68
14.50	47	6.07	48.00	157	5.80	67.50	221	5.54	87.00	285	5.27
15.00	49	2.56	48.50	159	1.48	68.00	223	1.22	87.50	207	0.95
15.50	50	10.24	49.00	160	9.17	68.50	224	8.90	88.00	288	8.64
16.00	52	55.93	49.50	162	4.86	69.00	226	4.59	88.50	290	4.32
16.50	54	1.61	50.00	164	0.55	69.50	228	0.29	89.00	292	0.01
17.00	55	9.30	50.50	165	8.24	70.00	229	7.97	89.50	293	7.69
17.50	57	4.98	51.00	167	3.92	70.50	231	3.65	90.00	295	3.38
18.00	59	0.68	51.50	168	11.60	71.00	232	11.34	90.50	296	11.06
18.50	60	8.36	52.00	170	7.29	71.50	234	7.02	91.00	298	6.75
19.00	62	4.05	52.50	172	2.97	72.00	236	2.71	91.50	300	2.43
19.50	63	11.74	53.00	173	10.66	72.50	237	10.40	92.00	301	10.12
20.00	65	7.42	53.50	175	6.34	73.00	239	6.08	92.50	303	5.80
20.50	67	3.14	54.00	177	2.03	73.50	241	1.77	93.00	305	1.49
									93.50	306	9.17

TABLE 2

M.	Ft.	Ins.	M.	Ft.	Ins.	M.	Ft.	Ins.	M.	Ft.	Ins.
.01		.39	.13		5.12	.25		9.84	.37	1	2.56
.02		.79	.14		5.51	.26		10.23	.38	1	2.96
.03		1.18	.15		5.91	.27		10.62	.39	1	3.35
.04		1.57	.16		6.30	.28		11.02	.40	1	3.74
.05		1.97	.17		6.69	.29		11.41	.41	1	4.13
.06		2.36	.18		7.09	.30		11.81	.42	1	4.53
.07		2.75	.19		7.48	.31	1	0.20	.43	1	4.92
.08		3.15	.20		9.87	.32	1	0.60	.44	1	5.31
.09		3.54	.21		8.26	.33	1	0.90	.45	1	5.71
.10		3.94	.22		8.66	.34	1	1.38	.46	1	6.10
.11		4.33	.23		9.05	.35	1	1.78	.47	1	6.49
.12		4.73	.24		9.44	.36	1	2.17	.48	1	6.89
									.49	1	7.28

EXAMPLE

To convert 47.72 metres to feet and inches:
Table 1

47.50m = 155 ft. 10.11 ins.

Table 2

0.22m =   8.66 ins.

155 ft. 18.77 ins.
= 156 ft. 6.77 ins.

TIME CONVERSIONS FOR ATHLETIC EVENTS

To convert times of races in metric distances into equivalent times for customary distances in yards, make the following conversions:

100 metres to 100 yds. — Subtract 0.9 seconds
200 metres to 220 yds. — Add 0.1 second
400 metres to 440 yds. — Add 0.3 second
800 metres to 880 yds. — Add 0.6 second
1,500 metres to 1 mile   — Add 18 seconds
5,000 metres to 3 miles   — Subtract 27 seconds
10,000 metres to 6 miles   — Subtract 55 seconds

TIME CONVERSIONS FOR SWIMMING EVENTS

Event	Add for Men	Add for Women
	in Secs.	
100m to 110 yds Freestyle	0.3	0.4
200m to 220 yds Freestyle	0.8	1.0
400m to 440 yds Freestyle	1.7	1.9
800m to 880 yds Freestyle	—	4.0
1500m to 1650 yds Freestyle	8.0	—
100m to 110 yds Backstroke	0.4	0.5
200m to 220 yds Backstroke	1.0	1.1
100m to 110 yds Breaststroke	0.6	0.7
200m to 220 yds Breaststroke	1.0	1.1
100m to 110 yds Butterfly	0.4	0.5
200m to 220 yds Butterfly	0.9	1.2
200m to 220 yds Individual Medley	0.9	1.1
400m to 440 yds Individual Medley	1.9	2.1

WEIGHTLIFTING CONVERSIONS

Kilos.	Lbs.	Kilos.	Lbs.	Kilos.	Lbs.	Kilos.	Lbs.
25	55	90	$198\frac{1}{4}$	$137\frac{3}{4}$	303	185	$407\frac{3}{4}$
45	99	$92\frac{1}{2}$	$203\frac{3}{4}$	140	$308\frac{1}{2}$	$187\frac{1}{2}$	$413\frac{1}{4}$
$47\frac{1}{2}$	$104\frac{1}{2}$	95	$209\frac{1}{4}$	$142\frac{1}{2}$	314	190	$418\frac{3}{4}$
50	110	$97\frac{1}{2}$	$214\frac{3}{4}$	145	$319\frac{1}{4}$	$192\frac{1}{2}$	$424\frac{1}{4}$
$52\frac{1}{2}$	$115\frac{1}{2}$	100	$220\frac{1}{4}$	$147\frac{1}{2}$	325	195	$429\frac{3}{4}$
55	$121\frac{1}{4}$	$102\frac{1}{2}$	$225\frac{3}{4}$	150	$330\frac{1}{2}$	$197\frac{1}{2}$	$435\frac{1}{4}$
$57\frac{1}{2}$	$126\frac{3}{4}$	105	$231\frac{1}{4}$	$152\frac{1}{2}$	336	200	$440\frac{3}{4}$
60	$132\frac{1}{4}$	$107\frac{1}{2}$	$236\frac{3}{4}$	155	$341\frac{1}{2}$	$202\frac{1}{2}$	$446\frac{1}{4}$
$62\frac{1}{2}$	$137\frac{3}{4}$	110	$242\frac{1}{2}$	$157\frac{1}{2}$	347	205	$451\frac{3}{4}$
65	$143\frac{1}{4}$	$112\frac{1}{2}$	248	160	$352\frac{1}{2}$	$207\frac{1}{2}$	$457\frac{1}{4}$
$67\frac{1}{2}$	$148\frac{3}{4}$	115	$253\frac{1}{2}$	$162\frac{1}{2}$	358	210	$462\frac{3}{4}$
70	$154\frac{1}{4}$	$117\frac{1}{2}$	259	165	$363\frac{3}{4}$	$212\frac{1}{2}$	$468\frac{1}{4}$
$72\frac{1}{2}$	$159\frac{3}{4}$	120	$264\frac{1}{2}$	$167\frac{1}{2}$	$369\frac{1}{4}$	215	$473\frac{3}{4}$
75	$165\frac{1}{4}$	$122\frac{1}{2}$	270	170	$374\frac{3}{4}$	$217\frac{1}{2}$	$479\frac{1}{4}$
$77\frac{1}{2}$	$170\frac{3}{4}$	125	$275\frac{1}{2}$	$172\frac{1}{2}$	$380\frac{1}{4}$	220	485
80	$176\frac{1}{4}$	$127\frac{1}{2}$	281	175	$385\frac{3}{4}$	$222\frac{1}{2}$	$490\frac{1}{4}$
$82\frac{1}{2}$	$181\frac{3}{4}$	130	$286\frac{1}{2}$	$177\frac{1}{2}$	$391\frac{1}{4}$	225	496
85	$187\frac{1}{4}$	$132\frac{1}{2}$	292	180	$396\frac{3}{4}$	$227\frac{1}{2}$	$501\frac{1}{4}$
$87\frac{1}{2}$	$192\frac{3}{4}$	135	$297\frac{1}{2}$	$182\frac{1}{2}$	$402\frac{1}{4}$	230	507

PROGRESS TABLE

	SPRING	SUMMER	AUTUMN
Form			
1st			
2nd			
3rd			
4th			
5th 6th			

TIMETABLE OF CLASSES

A.M.						
Time						
M						L
Tu						U
W						N
Th						C
F						H
S						

	P. M.			POST SCHOOL
L				
U				
N				
C				
H				

FINAL NOTE

As a final note on this handbook we would like to recommend that all Physical Education Teachers make a special point of reading the headings in the A - Z section which we have listed below.

THE EDITORS

ACCIDENTS

AGEING AND ADVANCEMENT

AIMS

AMATEUR STATUS

A.T.C.D.E.

B.A.O.L.P.E.

THE CENTRAL COUNCIL OF PHYSICAL RECREATION

DRUGS

FEET

FINANCE

INCOME TAX

IN-SERVICE TRAINING

INSURANCE

LEGALITY

THE PHYSICAL EDUCATION ASSOCIATION

QUALIFICATIONS

STUDENT SUPERVISION

VOCATION COURSES

APPENDIX VI